How to Become a Guitar Player from Hell

Jason Earls

Pleroma Publications

How to Become a Guitar Player from Hell

Copyright © 2007 by Jason Earls. *All rights reserved.* Unauthorized duplication is a violation of applicable laws.

ISBN 978-0-6151-5958-4

Cover and back cover, Copyright © 2007 by Jason Daniels. *All rights reserved.* Unauthorized duplication is a violation of applicable laws.

First Edition; September, 2007.
Pleroma Publications
RR 1 Box 43-5
Fritch, TX
79036
pleromapubs@cableone.net

Also by Jason Earls

Red Zen

Cocoon of Terror

If(Sid_Vicious == TRUE && Alan_Turing == TRUE) { ERROR_Cyberpunk(); }

0.13610152128364555667891105120136l5...

Contents

	Preface – Why a Guitar Player from Hell?	6
1	**Introductory Material**	8
	Level of This Book	9
	Brief History of the Guitar	10
	Tablature	11
	Knowing the Notes on Your Fretboard	15
	On Soloing	16
	A Good Way to Practice (Method One)	17
2	**Technique**	20
	Easy Scales – Minor Pentatonic and Blues	21
	Chords	23
	Bending Strings	26
	The Chromatic Scale	28
	Palm Muting	30
	Speed Picking	32
	Vibrato	35
	Rhythm Playing	37
	Taming the Fretboard with Modes	39
	String Dampening	43
	Double Stops	44
	Arpeggios	46
	Legato Playing	51
	Natural Harmonics	54
	String Skipping	56
	Staccato Playing and String Popping	59
	Developing Finger Strength	62
	Tremolo Picking	64
	One and Two Handed Tapping	66
	Artificial or Pinched Harmonics	71
	Bizarre Almost Uncontrollable Bends	72
	Extreme Lick #1	74
	Incorporating Open Strings	75
	Tremolo Bars & the Wah-Wham Technique	77
	Exotic Scales for Flair and Panache	79
	Muted Harmonics	84
	Finger Exercises	85
	Extreme Lick #2	88

	Mastering the Smaller Frets	90
	Outside Playing	92
	Alteration of the Pentatonic and Blues	96
	Finger Picking	97
	Extreme Lick #3	99
3	**Miscellaneous Advice**	**102**
	A Good Way to Practice (Method Two)	103
	On Equipment	105
	Improvisation	106
	On Bands	109
	Phrasing	111
	Taking Care of Your Hands	112
	String Care	112
	Organizing Band Rehearsals	113
	Listening	116
	Developing Your Own Style	118
	On Trios	119
	Ear Training	120
	Original Riffs	121
	Out-of-the-Box Exercise	122
	Finding the Right Key to Solo In	124
	Performing Live	125
	Necessary Tools for Working on the Guitar	126
	Imitation and Call & Response	127
	How to Improve Your Rhythm	128
	How to Get Gigs	129
	Guitar Related Quotes	130
	Start a Revolution With Your Guitar	132
	Two Useful Software Tools	134
	In Summary	134
	About the Author	136
	About the Artist	137

Preface – Why a Guitar Player from Hell?

One Halloween night in the early 90s, my band at the time, *Tainted Angel* – (I know, the name is far from wonderful) – were playing at a small bar in the Midwest called *Hoorahs* and we ended up setting a record that night for number of people in attendance: 365. We also made more money than we ever had previously (the cover charge was only a dollar per person, so we didn't get rich). It was our third gig together as a band and we were getting a great reaction from the crowd. A large group of college students were slam-dancing violently in the tiny dance area and causing quite a scene. They would applaud and yell after each song and it made us feel great and gave us plenty of energy since the physical conditions of the bar were pretty harsh.

The air was filled with too much tobacco smoke and the large crowd made the bar cramped and the temperature must have been well over 100 degrees. We also didn't have a stage to play on – we had to set up our equipment in one corner of the small dance floor. Our singer was having coughing attacks between songs from the abundance of nicotine floating through the air and at one point he came over and said he could barely breathe and that his eyes were stinging. I handed him a towel from my guitar case and he quickly wiped the sweat and smoke from his face, then went back and grabbed his microphone.

Only fifteen minutes into our first set, my amplifier overheated and completely shut down. We asked one of the waitresses carrying drinks if she could bring us a fan. Any kind of fan. She searched in the supply room and found one, carried it back and we propped it up behind the head of my amplifier to keep it cool.

The people we hired to run their sound board for us, a very nice middle-aged couple, became quite worried about the slam-dancing students in the dance area. They thought they were going to damage their expensive monitors setting at the edge of the dance floor. So they decided to stand directly in front of us with their arms held out and hands clasped together, their large bodies forming a barrier as we played on doing our best not to laugh since they had such worried looks on their faces and their bodies with their arms sticking out seemed both sad and humorous.

By the third set, I had already played the Eric Johnson instrumental "Cliffs of Dover" about eight times since many of the college kids in the audience were requesting it (even though they never tipped me once). Then after the third set ended – we always played four, 45-minute sets – I felt exhausted and a little relieved that the gig was almost over and I began making my way toward the bar for a cold glass of water.

At the half way point in the thick drunken crowd, a hard-looking woman of about 40 came up and complimented me on my guitar playing. I said, "thank you very much, ma'am" and suddenly she raised her arms and tried to hug me while puckering her lips and moving forward to kiss me. She was obviously intoxicated and I placed my index and middle fingers on her forehead and gently pushed her lips away and continued walking toward the bar for my water.

Our bass player, Mike, was soon standing behind me at the bar and as I took a long drink of the cool refreshing water I heard one of his friends whom I had never met come up and begin talking to him. His first two sentences to Mike were, "You guys sound great tonight, man. And your guitar player is from hell."

It was the best compliment I had ever received.

That is the story behind the title of this book.

My main goal is that after you finish reading it, anyone who hears you play will also think you're a guitar player from hell.

1
Introductory Material

Level of this Book

This book is not intended for absolute beginners. What I mean by "absolute" is that it is not an introductory book for learning how to play the guitar from the very beginning stages. Instead, it is mainly a collection of chapters on various techniques, licks, chords, and tips that I think are necessary for someone to greatly improve their guitar playing ability, and which are guaranteed to be effective if practiced enough.

For the most part, I have assumed readers of this book are familiar with the overall rudiments of playing the guitar (although I will cover many basic topics here and there). For example, I expect that you already know the difference between an acoustic and an electric guitar, that you are familiar with the names of the parts of your instrument, that you know the proper way to hold your guitar and strum it, that you know a number of standard chords and have memorized a few rudimentary scales, that you know how to tune your guitar and put on new strings, and also how to jump off a drum riser, do a somersault and land on your feet while bashing out an F# minor barre chord (only kidding about that last one).

Although I will cover a few basic topics in this book, I recommend that if you are still at the very beginning stages of playing, you put this book up for a few months to a year and develop a good foundation first from either a teacher or another book more devoted to the absolute basics, then you can return to this text with more ease and confidence in understanding the material presented within.

With that said, I must also say that the *basic playing techniques* are very important. You will never get away from the basics because they always work. For example, a simple E to A based chord progression or riff, with a change to C and G for a chorus section, then a solo section in which you employ only a minor pentatonic scale will always sound good no matter what your playing level. Mastering any basic technique and thinking about why and how it works and then pushing it to another level is a great methodology and philosophy to have and follow.

Mainly, I am aiming this book at intermediate level electric guitarists by providing many intermediate lessons, but also adding in a lot of basic and advanced concepts as well. The type of music I will be covering will mostly be rock-n-roll, "heavy metal," and blues playing, with a small amount of jazz also discussed.

My overriding goal is to give you useful methods and tips to help you break through to another level of proficiency on the instrument. In every chapter I will attempt to provide detailed explanations of certain topics with key pieces of information that took me years to learn, with at least one piece of "advanced" information that not many players know about. It could be a better way of holding your hands to execute a difficult chord voicing, or an experimental bending technique that I have never seen anyone use before, or a new way of operating the tremolo bar and wah-wah pedal simultaneously, or simply a different philosophy or "out-of-the-box" thinking method for the way you approach the guitar, all of which will hopefully improve your playing considerably. Whatever it may be I want to give you genuine "insider" information in as many chapters as possible, with as much "secret" knowledge that came from my own struggles and experiences learning the guitar which I have never seen explained anywhere else. (In some chapters it will not be possible to include any "secret" information, but in most it will.)

Also, you do not have to read this book from the first page to the last. You can skip around since the chapters are not in sequential order. If you have a short amount of time on any particular day, you can dip in at some point and hopefully come away with a useful technique to add to your guitar arsenal.

Many of the chapters are short because I did not want to bog the reader down with excessive verbiage or a plethora of examples. Most guitarists like something to be left to the imagination, or would rather be playing their guitars or inventing and extending new licks instead of sitting around reading books. I also did not go into any deep discussions of musical theory underlying each concept. A little bit is offered here and there, but not too much since I wanted to leave many things open and not get slowed down by excessive theoretical detail, which most rock players simply ignore anyway. (Again, it is possible to think of this book as simply a collection of techniques, tips, and overall advice on various guitar methods if that is more desirable.)

Also, I will include a lot of practical advice tangential to actually playing the guitar. For example, I will talk about how to find band members, how to get gigs, what kind of guitar picks and strings may be suitable for you, information on organizing band rehearsals, some necessary tools for working on your guitar, other equipment tips and general advice along with personal anecdotes and brief mentions of famous guitarists and also music that has influenced me, among other topics.

The best result I could hope for is that every serious, gigging, guitar player keeps a copy of this book in their guitar case at all times.

Brief History of the Guitar

As I'm sure most readers already know, the guitar is one of the most popular instruments in the world. It is generally considered the "coolest" instrument in a band, and second only to the singer. Every year thousands of teenagers and even adults strap on guitars and bash out their first E chords pretending to be rock gods. Although many people begin the journey of learning the guitar, most give up after a short time since it is a long arduous process to becoming a proficient or professional musician.

Have you ever wondered where the guitar came from? What its exact origins are and who actually invented it? The guitar was first mentioned in written records around the year 1300 A.D. But at this early stage, guitars consisted of only four doubled-up strings and resembled lutes more than they did the instruments we know today. We have evidence that the Malago people of Spain actually invented the guitar, but no one is certain others didn't create it before them. Around 1770, a sixth string was added and the guitar finally received its basic form that we use now.

Luthiers are craftsmen who make guitars and repair them, and a few continue to make innovations and modifications to the guitar today. I've seen guitars with seven strings (one either lower or higher than the normal six); guitars with scalloped fretboards; acoustics with two sets of strings – one running across the soundhole of the instrument, the other in the normal position running down the fretboard – I've seen double necked guitars; 12-string guitars – the normal six with doubles an octave higher – and the list goes on. Perhaps in another hundred years modern electric guitars will be so entirely different from what we know today we won't even recognize them as guitars. Or perhaps another instrument will come along and replace the electric guitar entirely, rendering it obsolete. It could happen.

Nevertheless, the electric guitar is still an incredibly popular and wonderfully expressive instrument, well worth your time and energy.

(For the purposes of this book, I will be dealing strictly with the common six-string electric guitar in a standard tuning of E, A, D, G, B, and E.)

Tablature

Tablature is the system of notation used for displaying music in this book. Before I define it exactly, you should know it will be a simplified version of tablature – an ASCII based system. The tablature that appears in popular guitar magazines is usually a little fancier. Also, I won't be discussing or explaining any type of traditional musical notation (you don't have to know how to read music to play the guitar) so I won't include any musical notes above the tablature that are normally seen in instructional books, since one of my goals is to keep things as simple as possible. One way to do that and also save space is to focus on an ASCII based tablature system instead of common musical notation when denoting chords and melodies on the guitar.

Tablature (often shortened to just "tab") is a system of notation quick and easy to learn. It was invented in Europe around the 1300s and is intended mainly for fretted instruments – ukulele, bass, mandolin, lute, banjo, and of course guitar – but denoting music of other non-fretted instruments is also possible (drums, for instance).

I do know how to read music, but I will admit I'm slow and occasionally make mistakes. Tablature is much easier and quicker to understand.

Many musicians and famous guitar players in history could not read music, the great jazz player, Django Reinhardt, being one example. Although I won't explain how to read music in this book, I believe it is still highly beneficial to learn to do so, and I recommend at some point in your guitar study that you obtain a copy of a good book on music theory and learn to read music well.

To reiterate, we will be using a simple ASCII based method of guitar tablature in this book. Occasionally I will have to denote bends, hammer-ons, pull-offs, taps, slides, etc., but whenever possible I will explain those things in the text above so the tablature will appear "clean" and clutter free. Here is how our tablature will look:

```
e|---x---0---3----|
B|---2---1---0----|
G|---2---0---0----|
D|---2---2---0----|
A|---0---3---2----|
E|-----------3----|
    A   C   G
```

It is quite simple and intuitive – I'm sure most of you are already familiar with tab. Nevertheless here is an explanation: Each string of the guitar is layed out horizontally. The lowest string, E, is at the bottom and the highest, e (using a lowercase to show it's an octave higher) is at the top. The other strings when using a standard tuning are A, D, G, and B. (You should memorize this string pattern because from now on I will not put the names of the strings beside the tablature.) Notice that the system is reversed, or upside down, from how your strings normally look when someone is holding your guitar and you are observing them.

Three chords are listed above: A, C, and G. A '3' on a line means you are to press down on the third fret on that particular string and pick the note to sound it, while an '0' means an open string is to be played, and an 'x' means no note is to be played on that string (or, it can be hit but should be muffled or muted with a finger or your palm). When all the notes appear in a straight vertical line as above, you are to strum them. Simple. Also, I will occasionally place numbers underneath to specify which fingers are best to use for a specific passage, but they are only suggestions, you may find that using other fingers is more comfortable. The fingering key will be 1 – index finger, 2 – middle finger, 3 – ring finger, and 4 – pinky or smallest finger. With tablature, it is much easier to visualize how things are to be played since it is meant to be a representation of your instrument's fretboard.

How to Become a Guitar Player from Hell

An even simpler way to denote chords is horizontally, like this, (which shouldn't require any explanation):

```
      D              Em             B5
x x 0 2 3 2    0 2 2 0 0 x    x 2 4 4 x x
```

A standard D chord, an E minor chord, and a B power chord are displayed above.

Things get a little more complicated when we start denoting solos or single note lines. Bends, hammer-ons, trills, pull-offs, ghost bends, slides, raked notes, all of these can by designated with tablature by using certain letters or symbols between, or in front of, the notes. For example, here is how a common full step bend will be listed:

```
|---------|
|---------|
|-14b16---|
|---------|
|---------|
|---------|
```

So you can see that our tablature is stripped down and minimal, providing only the "meat" and avoiding any excess clutter.

A basic (yet thorough) outline of the material will be given in the text and in tablature form so you can learn it in a manner that suits you.

Freedom and simplicity will be major components of my instructional method.

For another example of a performance related designation, here is how a G power chord *sliding* up to an A power chord will look:

```
|--------|
|--------|
|-7s9----|
|-5s7----|
|--------|
|--------|
```

And here is a more complicated lick:

```
         ~                          ~
|---------------------------------------|
|---------------------------------------|
|-7b9--7--5--7--5--4h5h7p5p4h5h7p5p4s2---|
|---------------------------------------|
|---------------------------------------|
|---------------------------------------|
```

How to Become a Guitar Player from Hell

This lick explained in words is, first, using your ring finger, bend the D note on your G string up two frets to the E note and apply a little vibrato, then play D, C, D, C, with your index and ring fingers using an almost staccato feel (short choppy notes, not letting them ring out) then shift your first finger down to the B note on the 4th fret and using your index, middle and pinky fingers play the B, C, and D notes as fast and smooth as you can using only hammer-ons and pull-offs, then slide your index finger down to the A note on the second fret and apply vibrato there. Done. The hammer-ons and pull-offs often clutter the tablature up a bit, so whenever possible I will leave them out by explaining certain performance designations in the text itself. For example, when discussing tapping methods, instead of listing this:

```
      T         T         T         T         T~
|------------------------------------------------|
|------------------------------------------------|
|-18p12h15h18p12h15h18p12h15h18p12h15h20----|
|------------------------------------------------|
|------------------------------------------------|
|------------------------------------------------|
```

I will probably list this simplified version instead, which is much easier to read:

```
      T         T         T         T         T
|------------------------------------------------|
|------------------------------------------------|
|-18-12-15-18-12-15-18-12-15-18-12-15-20----|
|------------------------------------------------|
|------------------------------------------------|
|------------------------------------------------|
```

And it will be understood that all notes are to be either hammered-on, pulled-off, or tapped.

So you can see it is much easier to use tablature to denote licks and chords on the guitar than it is to use words. The only major drawback with tablature is that the timing and rhythm of how things are phrased cannot be adequately conveyed most of the time. So to learn a new song and to make sure you are getting the rhythms and phrasing exactly right, often you will have to listen to the song first before looking at the tablature. (The timing of most of the original phrases and chords in this book can be adapted to suit your taste, so it isn't important that you hear them before learning them from the tablature.)

Here is a short tablature key that covers most of the symbols used in this book. A few common electric guitar techniques are not included in the legend below, such as tapped harmonics, volume swells, ghost bends, prebends, and tremolo bar manipulations, but I will be discussing a few of those things in depth in other chapters and the tablature symbols for those will not be needed as much.

Key to Tablature

----

    b - **bend**
    h - **hammer-on**
    p - **pull-off**
    s - **slide**
    ~ - **vibrato**
    r - **release**
    T - **tap**
    [h] - **artificial harmonic**
    <n> - **natural harmonic**
    tr - **trill**
    /// - **tremolo picking**
    PM - **palm mute**

There will be a lot more musical examples given with tablature in this book, and any time a new concept is introduced that has not already appeared, be assured that it will be fully explained.

Knowing the Names of the Notes on Your Fretboard

It has been assumed that you already know the names of the notes on your instrument, or how to locate them, but if for some reason you do not know, I will explain the simple process.

First of all, musical notes follow this pattern, which you should memorize:

A, A#/B♭, B, C, C#/D♭, D, D#/E♭, E, F, F#/G♭, G, G#/A♭, A, ...

If you don't know what A#/B♭ means, it is only that A# or 'A sharp' is the same as B♭ or 'B flat'– the notes are equivalent. Also notice there is no B# or E# in the pattern. I don't know why.

Once you have the pattern memorized, all you have to do to find the name of a certain note on your fretboard is recall the names of your guitar strings E, A, D, G, B, and high E, then start with a certain open string pitch and work your way up the frets, naming each note as you go, until you arrive at the note you want to know the name of. Simple.

How to Become a Guitar Player from Hell

Let's have an example. Say you want to know the name of the note on your G string at the 6th fret. Start with G in the open position, then continue with the pattern outlined above and work your way up. The first fret on the G string must be G# or A♭, then the second fret is A, then the third fret is A# or B♭. (Only three more frets to go.) Next is B, then C, and finally we arrive at the 6th fret, which is C#/D♭. I would call the note C# instead of D♭, I hardly ever refer to any notes on the guitar as "flat," since I never like to think I am playing flat in any way, which can be the same as "dull" or "lifeless."

So that is all there is to finding notes on your guitar. I admit I don't have all the notes memorized across the entire fretboard, although I do have most of the lower notes on the E and A strings memorized since they are regularly root notes of various chords, but I can find the names of notes in other positions on the fretboard very quickly.

Knowing the names of notes is essential for communicating with other musicians and also figuring out chord voicings and working out scales and modes to use for your solos.

On Soloing

In this text, much time and words will be spent discussing various *soloing* techniques. Although rhythm guitar playing is extremely important, in my opinion it takes much more practice to learn how to play good solos and keep up with modern techniques and execute them with consistency than it does to strum chords. Of course, by soloing techniques I mean the advanced ones such as speed picking, string skipping, fast legato patterns, tapping licks, trills, artificial harmonics and the use of exotic scales, among other concepts.

A brief aside: one of the first things that inspired me to pick up the guitar was seeing Edward Van Halen's solo on the song "5150" that appeared on their *Live Without A Net* video. The incredible techniques Eddie displayed, the tapping and fast pentatonic runs, the slow and atmospheric tapped slides on bent strings, the blazing legato patterns, all of it blew me away and I wanted to learn every impressive method he displayed in that solo. Ever since that time, playing great solos was always the most important thing about playing the guitar for me. Also, after seeing and hearing the "5150" solo (as I will explain more in the chapter on Rhythm Guitar), I almost ignored rhythm guitar playing for a couple of years when I shouldn't have. But my point here is that much of the focus of this book will be on various advanced soloing techniques that crop up in the rock and metal categories, with a few jazz methods thrown in as well.

The reason I was always more interested in soloing instead of playing rhythm guitar or memorizing hundreds of different chord voicings to merely back up a singer or to strum mildly along with the drummer was not due to some kind of egotistical character trait. Rather, I always felt that soloing was similar to going on a journey of exploration and seeing what interesting musical phrases I could invent or create along the way. A good solo to me is a process of discovery and improvisation is instant musical creation and the most exciting part of making music, in my opinion. Self-expression, invention, improvisation, mining unexplored territory, taking forbidden journeys into the beyond, these things represent freedom to me. Perhaps when jazz players perform chord solos they feel the same way. I can't really say.

Another remark on soloing: as time went on, and I learned more about how to play the guitar and became more interested in improvisation, I noticed that whenever I would practice every day, playing for many hours, my ideas during improvisational solos would become rather stale and uninspired, as if I were merely playing the same licks repeatedly. But if I did not practice very much during one particular day, or even skipped a couple of days of playing altogether, even though my technique would go down quite a bit and I would play sloppily, whenever it came time to improvise my ideas would be fresh and alive and exciting and it would seem like I was playing entirely new phrases and melodies that I'd never heard anywhere else. Maybe other players are different, maybe they don't have this problem of getting stale from too much practice, but at least for me, I had to choose which quality was more important: fresh ideas while improvising and a lower level of technique; or practicing a lot for enhanced execution, then having rather stale improvisational ideas.

A Good Way to Practice - (Method One)

You must practice a lot to become a good guitar player. There is no other way to learn. It is not easy to build excellent technique, it takes a lot of time and effort, and if you do not continue to practice you will quickly lose your ability to play sophisticated scales, arpeggios, and licks in a precise fashion; any technique that you have built up will almost disappear for most people as soon as they stop playing for even a short amount of time, although you won't entirely lose everything.

When I first began playing guitar seriously I set myself a (rather harsh) practice schedule of five hours a day (this was in the summers and when I had no job) and I was able to stick to it most of the time. A year or two later I increased it to seven or eight hours a day, but sometimes only got in five. This is moderately extreme. When you first start out, you should try to have two thirty-minute practice sessions per day. It is not really the duration of the practice session that is important, but the frequency. It is much better to have shorter sessions of playing once or twice daily, than to engage in one long practice session only on Sundays, for example. Consistency is the main ingredient. You are training your fingers and hands but also your brain to absorb the patterns of how to play the guitar, so it is better to not go for long periods of time without playing anything.

Patience is also a must. If you can't play something on a certain day, don't get discouraged. Move on to something else and come back to it later. There were many times when I couldn't play a certain popular song from the tablature that I really wanted to learn and it would make me feel depressed and miserable. But after continuing to practice other things for a few weeks, I could usually return to the previous song I had trouble with and be able to play it from beginning to end. So again, always try to develop your patience. I have known a few unruly people in my life who have struggled to learn a new riff and because they couldn't play it well enough on the first try they would smash their guitars against a wall. That is not recommended. Also, try not to practice in a cold environment. Your fingers will be stiff and it may be quite painful to play.

My practice method during the longer sessions was simple. I would partition the hours into thirty minute segments in which I would focus on one particular topic. Most often I would begin with finger exercises for thirty minutes, then I might work on some difficult chord progressions with challenging voicings, perhaps I would move on to string skipping next, then I would continue with some tapping exercises, or if I was in a band at the time I might work on writing a new riff or bridge section of music, maybe work out a new solo... Those practice sessions were a lot of fun. Sometimes I would stray off-topic into various things in the middle of my thirty minute sessions and get carried away playing whatever I wanted, but when I found myself doing this I would try to pull my attention back to the task at hand. Usually I would end the practice session by playing along to various songs that I liked – jamming to my favorite bands on tape or CD was probably the most enjoyable part of the session, I will discuss a practice method related to learning new songs in this manner in another chapter.

(Another aspect of guitar playing that I sort of neglected when I was learning is finger style playing, which I will also explain in a later chapter. I never really liked picking with my fingers. I was always more of a rock player who wanted to use a plectrum and wail away with heavy distortion. But don't follow my example. You should practice finger picking and become proficient at it.)

Also during these practice session I wouldn't just put in my time, I would set goals for myself, such as executing a troublesome lick more cleanly than I had during the last practice session, or I would strive to add at least one new technique or chord to my repertoire. Also I'd regularly use a metronome during my sessions, which are great for increasing accuracy and speed.

Again, I encourage you to be patient with learning to play the guitar and any new techniques involved. Don't get discouraged if you can't play something on the first attempt and throw your guitar into the river. It takes time to learn to play well.

I recommend starting out with one hour of practice for five or six days a week, splitting it up into two thirty minute sessions if you need to (say before and after work or school), and if you stick to this regimen for a couple of years and consciously try to improve and not just play around, you will see dramatic improvement. Then if you want to take your playing to a higher level, you will most likely have to increase your practice time to three or four hours a day. But always strive to keep your practice sessions fun and entertaining without getting off track too often.

Now let's get started learning some guitar techniques.

2
Technique

Simple Scales – Minor Pentatonic and Blues

I love scales. All kinds of scales. Simple, complex, plain, exotic. It doesn't matter to me. I love them all. Some cultures consider single note melodies to be the essence of all music. They don't rely on a combination of notes played on a variety of instruments to build up extensive harmonies or overtones that most people won't even be able to hear or appreciate. Usually they consider the melody to be enough. I agree with them. Although it is important to consider what chords your melodies are played over, it is still the melody that is the most important thing in music to me. And what is the foundation of melodies? Scales.

We will encounter many type of scales in this book at different points. I am going to sprinkle them through the text like diamonds and they will become more exotic as the book progresses. We will start off with one of the simplest and most useful scales in music. The minor pentatonic scale. I will then give you a few easy licks to perform. Here is the minor pentatonic scale in the key of G:

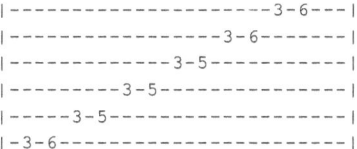

The notes are G, A#, C, D, F, before it repeats with the G an octave higher. Notice it has only five notes before it hits the octave again. Penta means five. Pentatonic scale. It is a very important scale that turns up in many different cultures all over the world. You will encounter this scale a million times while playing the guitar and learning new songs. North Americans are familiar with this scale because of its extensive use in American blues music. But even the French composer Claude Debussy employed the pentatonic scale in his unique compositions. (I suspect most readers are already familiar with the minor pentatonic.)

When playing this scale, most players rely on their index and ring fingers. But for the notes on the sixth fret I recommend you use your pinky finger. The little finger or pinky finger is difficult to build strength in, so you should use it anytime an opportunity arises to make it stronger.

The minor pentatonic is very easy to improvise with, which is one reason it turns up in so many disparate parts of the world. If you haven't experimented with the minor pentatonic before, I suggest you start improvising with it immediately, playing notes in different places and making up your own blues licks. Then you can string together everything you know to create a solo. Here is a common rock lick that relies on the minor pentatonic:

```
|-3---------3---------3---------3------------|
|---6p3-------6p3-------6p3-------6p3--------|
|-------5b7-------5b7-------5b7-------5b7----|
|--------------------------------------------|
|--------------------------------------------|
|--------------------------------------------|
```

In words, so that the tablature is clear: play the high G note with your index finger, then fret the 6th fret with your pinky finger and pull off to your index on the 3rd fret, then using your ring finger, bend the G string at the 5th fret up two frets, or a whole step. Practice it slowly at first, then using a metronome, gradually build up speed. This is a common lick that pops up in a thousand songs.

Now to bring the standard minor pentatonic up a notch, we can kick into something more difficult such as the following lick to show people we are truly guitar players from hell.

```
|-18p15-20p15-------------18p15-20p15-------------|
|------------18p15-------------------18p15--------|
|------------------17b19-------------------17b19-|
|-------------------------------------------------|
|-------------------------------------------------|
|-------------------------------------------------|
```

This lick has a little bit of a stretch to it, but it's still from the minor pentatonic. To play the pull-off from the C at the 20th fret to the G at the 15th fret, you will most definitely have to use your pinky. Then for the pull off on the B string, I use my ring finger and then bend the C note on the 17th fret G string with my middle finger up a full step. That is how I execute this lick and think that fingering is best for obtaining maximum speed.

Next we move on to the blues blues scale, which is closely related to the pentatonic. Simply add one note to the minor pentatonic, the flatted fifth, which is C#, to get the blues scale in G:

```
|-------------------------3-6----|
|----------------------3-6-------|
|----------------3-5-6-----------|
|-----------3-5------------------|
|-----3-4-5----------------------|
|-3-6----------------------------|
```

The flatted fifth provides the "blue note" (although it is possible to add other blue notes – some players add the flatted 7th or major 3rd – but most commonly you will see the minor pentatonic with a flatted 5th referred to as the blues scale).

Here is a lick using the notes of the blues scale that I love to play live. I play it as fast as possible, striving for 32nd or 64th notes.

```
|--------------------------------------|--------------------|
|-15----------------15-----------------|-15-----------------|
|----18-17-15-17-18----18-17-15-17-18-|----18-17-15-17-18--|
|--------------------------------------|--------------------|
|--------------------------------------|--------------------|
|--------------------------------------|--------------------|
```

The "blue" note occurs on the G string at the 18th fret. Also notice this lick falls perfectly on the fretboard for extremely fast playing.

So there you have two of the most basic scales in music, the minor pentatonic and the blues scale, with a few basic licks to get you started (I will provide much more sophisticated licks and phrases as the book progresses). There is also a major pentatonic scale but it will not be discussed much in this book since I am not too fond of the way it sounds.

Chords

Having a large chord vocabulary is a valuable and important thing for any guitarist, but for rock and metal genres you will not need to know as many chords as say, a jazz player will. Since rock players usually play with distortion on their amps to create a heavy or sustained tone, many sophisticated chord voicings will simply not be heard, which is why power chords (those that consist of only the root note and the fifth) are so common in rock-n-roll and heavy metal styles of music.

Nevertheless, you should still try to learn as many chords as you can and develop an extensive chord vocabulary. Occasionally you may find yourself using a clean tone for a particular song and then you will be able to use more elaborate voicings, which *will* be heard in the music.

It is already assumed you know many of the standard chords, but for reference I have included many of the most common ones below.

A chord is simply a collection of notes played simultaneously. They can consist of notes from all six strings, or can be made up of only two notes, which are again usually called power chords. Since I was always more of a rock or metal guitar player, I never delved too deeply into the extremely complex types of chord voicings. Most of the time, because of the kinds of bands I was in, I would usually play power chords along with the standard C, G, E, A, and D chords. For a long time that was the extent of my chord vocabulary, and it worked out reasonably well and I was fine with it, even though now I know I should have learned as many chords as possible right from the start.

In jazz and a few other forms of music, there are such things as chord solos, which can be truly amazing. That is, there are jazz players who can play long passages based entirely around chord clusters and they sound incredible and inspirational. I wish I had the ability to play chord solos, I have much respect for any player who can, but I am not a jazz player and I probably never will be. I like to use distortion on my amplifier frequently, and an overdriven amp simply doesn't work well for playing chord solos.

It is assumed most readers of this text already know many of the standard chords and how to play barre chords, but I am going to include a few below for reference. Some of the more unusual or "advanced" chords will be listed that have slightly more elaborate voicings than those normally employed in rock settings. There is no important reason I chose the chords that follow other than they sound good to me. I won't include a lot of theory behind the chords, such as where the seventh or augmented notes are, or which note should be considered "inverted" or not. If any readers are interested in that type of analysis or overall chord theory and how tones can work together for different voicings, then I recommend getting a book devoted solely to that area and studying it. Quite honestly I don't feel qualified to delve into that type of discussion when there are others who have devoted their entire lives to studying chord shapes and how they work.

All right, first, starting with the simplest chord clusters, we will have power chords. These are usually played with only the root and fifth of the scale, but sometimes players will add the octave on top of the fifth. So an A power chord can be played like this:

```
    A
5 7 x x x x
```

Or this:

```
    A
5 7 7 x x x
```

For playing power chords other than A, you can simply keep your hand in the same shape and slide it around to other root notes to get different chords.

Here are a few basic standard chords in the ultra-simplified tablature format:

```
      C            G            D            A
x 3 2 0 1 0   3 2 0 0 0 3   x x 0 2 3 2   x 0 2 2 2 0
```

How to Become a Guitar Player from Hell

```
    Em              F               B
0 2 2 0 0 x     1 3 3 2 1 1     x 2 4 4 4 x
```

    Two tips I will give you about two of the chords above. Notice that the necessary fingering for the C major chord is, ring finger on the third fret, middle finger on the second fret, index finger on the first fret; we can make a barre chord out of this shape, move it around the fretboard to get other major chords, and they will still retain the nice sound produced by the shape. For example, you can play E major and D major like this

```
      E               D
x 7 6 4 5 4     x 5 4 2 3 2
```

    Notice those are the same shapes we used for our original C major chord, but using a different fingering. For example, to play the E major, we barre the notes on the 4th fret with our index fingers and play the other notes with our pinky, ring, and middle fingers where it seems obvious. This type of barre chord also works with the G major chord shape and the D major chord shape as well. I will leave it to you to work them out. This is one of the methods taught in the "CAGED" method of guitar playing (which I'm not well versed in, so it won't be discussed in depth).

    Two other chords of interest that you may want to add to your repertoire are suspended second chords:

```
    Asus2           Bsus2
x 0 2 2 0 0     x 2 4 4 2 2
```

    I love the sounds of these chords. To me they have a "mystical" or "transcendental" sound – (yes, those words may annoy some readers, but I guess I'm just a transcendental kind of guy.) There are also suspended fourth chords that sound quite nice, which I won't list here. The word "suspended" basically means the third of the chord has been eliminated and as a result there is a feeling of inherent "suspension" – that the chord should "resolve" soon, but it won't. You can move the basic suspended second shape around to get other chords of the same type.

```
    Gadd9           Aadd9
3 x 5 4 3 5     5 x 7 6 5 7
```

    With the major added ninth chords above, you fret the root note on the E string with your thumb, then mute the A string entirely by touching it lightly with the overlapping flesh of your thumb and ring finger, then you use your ring, middle, and index fingers to fret the middle notes while grabbing the highest note with your pinky on the high E string. The voicings of these chords sound very "Hendrixian," after Jimi Hendrix, since he used them quite a bit in his material.

Our final three chords are ones I use mainly for playing funk rhythms. They are pretty common. Move them around to get different roots and additional chords of the same type.

```
     E9            E13           E7#9
x 7 8 7 7 7    X 7 8 7 7 9    x 7 6 7 8 x
```

There are many other fingerings and voicings one can use for playing the standard major, minor, 7th, 9th, and other chords. But the chords above are mainly the ones I use the most. They have worked for me when playing many different styles of music. But don't limit yourself to them. Strive to increase your chord vocabulary as much as possible since you never know when you will need a certain unusual chord for an original song, or if you ever want to launch into an impromptu chord solo and hope the mystical forces of the universe will be there to guide you through a successful and transcendental journey into infinity.

Bending Strings

String bending is a technique used for making the guitar sound like the human voice. Probably every lead guitar player in the world regularly bends strings now, even most country players bend strings since it is such a common practice, although I did run into a country guitarist once who claimed he rarely had to change his strings because he didn't "bend them like spaghetti."

Since this book isn't intended for absolute beginners, I won't explain the basic technique behind string bending, but I will say there are many ways to bend strings (or maybe it should be there are many *degrees* to which you can bend strings) once you have the essential points down. There are also many ways to treat the notes after they have been bent.

To begin our exercises for this chapter, first place your third finger on a string, preferably the G string, and push it up one whole step, which is two frets, then apply some vibrato. This is probably the simplest and most commonly used bend (your ringer finger is usually the strongest, and with your index and middle fingers behind it, it becomes even stronger). But you don't have to be limited to this simple bend only.

We will move on to some wider interval bends in a moment, but first, use your third finger on the G string again and bend the string up, but this time only go a half step and apply no vibrato at all. How does it sound? Better with vibrato, right?

How to Become a Guitar Player from Hell

Next, bend the same note up one and a half steps and this time apply vibrato. If your fingers are particularly strong you can try to bend the note up two whole steps, which is four frets, or you can go even higher. Note that it will take a considerable amount of finger strength – and you may end up busting a few strings – to execute bends up to and beyond two steps. The blues guitarist Buddy Guy made this type of "extreme" bending famous and popularized it among guitarists; his fingers were so strong he really could bend strings like they were spaghetti.

Ghost bends are also possible. This is where you prebend the string up to a certain point without sounding the note, then strike it with your plectrum or pluck it and let the string fall back to its original position to release the bend. It is an interesting effect although I do not use it very often.

Microtonal bends are also interesting. This is where you bend the string only a quarter of a step, or just an eighth of a step away (if that is even audible), to give the note a small "twang" or "twinge" or "smear" that differs slightly from the original note. George Lynch, a guitarist who played with the band *Dokken* for many years, used microtonal bends frequently in his solos (he also had a wicked legato technique), and they were quite effective. Some guitarists such as Yngwie Malmsteen have scalloped fretboards and athough I have never played a guitar equipped with one, I believe they allow you to execute even more subtle microtonal bends.

Bending strings behind the nut of the guitar is also possible, although you will not be able to get particularly wide intervals in this way and you will not have nearly as much control over the notes.

There will be no tablature for our next exercise. It won't be necessary. I can describe it with words and it will be easy enough to follow. Here is one way to practice your bending prowess. First, bend a note up a half step on any string you want. Then play the note a half step up the regular way by fretting it and listening to make sure the intonation of the fretted note matches your previous bend perfectly. Next, bend a string up a full step, which is two frets, then check it by fretting it two frets up. Continue this "bend and check" method with higher and higher bends. You can also apply vibrato to the bent note, then fret the same note and apply some vibrato there. Listen to the differences in the sound of the vibrato. With the bent note it is going to occur below the note and then up to the proper pitch, while with the fretted note, the vibrato will be starting at the intended note and going up higher in pitch then dropping back down. You'll see what I mean when you observe the two different types of vibrato carefully as you play them. After practicing the "bend and check" method using wider and wider intervals, give your fingers a short rest (you may want to play a few scales to work some blood into your fingers), then move to a different string and begin again. You can also bend a note up a full step, then let it fall down to a half step and apply your vibrato there. Experiment with different bending methods and try many different things. Be sure to use different positions of the neck for practicing your bends also. Up very high and down extremely low.

Before I forget, John McLaughlin was another guitarist who used scalloped fretboards and when he was in a band called Shakti which he formed with Indian classical players, he would perform very strange sounding wide-interval bends that involved plenty of microtones. For example, judging from the tape I had of McLaughlin playing, in one instance it seemed he bent a string up about 1 1/2 steps, then let the note fall a half step, then without picking it again he bent the note 2 full steps, then let it fall down to 1/2 step from the original note, and in between he would be hitting and milking a few microtonal notes as well as adding subtle and wide vibrato here and there – very unusual and dynamic bends that almost had a sitar like quality. Surely his scalloped fretboard helped him achieve these exotic and wonderful bends as well.

Remember that when bending, you should let your ears take over and be your guide to the notes you want to hit, which means that practicing bends may also improve your ear.

The Chromatic Scale

Chromatic means moving up or down in pitch by consecutive half steps so that all 12 notes are played. The chromatic scale is a nice finger exercise when played on guitar and can also open up your ears (or destroy your sense of pitch, however you want to look at it) to tones other than the common chordal and scalar tones normally used in solos. Regular 'in-key' notes of the standard major and minor scales can become quite stale if played continuously, and you should know that there are never any wrong notes in music. Any tone can be played against any background collection of pitches in any order at any time, which is what makes the chromatic scale possible. There is no right or wrong in music, anything goes. There aren't any laws or limits, only your individual ears to tell you what sounds good or not.

You can combine the chromatic scale with other scales, shift in and out of them, play pentatonic and chromatic, dorian and mixoldyian with chromatic, bebop dominant and chromatic, any scale at all, transition in and out of the scales and modes or blend them together to create timeless and otherworldly musical phrases no other living being or extraterrestrial has ever played before on this planet. Incorporating the chromatic scale into your improvisations can be very exciting. Here is the chromatic scale beginning at the 5th position for your education and delectation:

How to Become a Guitar Player from Hell

```
|------------------|------------------|----------1-2-3-4---|
|------------------|------------------|-2-3-4-5------------|
|------------------|----------2-3-4-5-|--------------------|
|------------------|-3-4-5-6----------|--------------------|
|----------4-5-6-7-|------------------|--------------------|
|-5-6-7-8----------|------------------|--------------------|
```

Notice how we are simply playing consecutive notes with all four fingers on one string, then shifting up to the next string but moving back one fret and continuing the 1-2-3-4 finger pattern. You will use this basic pattern for every string except when going between the G and B strings where you will stay in the same position. The chromatic scale is fun to play and also a good technique builder.

Most musicians and musicologists consider so called "wrong" notes or pitches that are out of key to be "passing" tones, which are pitches played rather quickly and "passed over" on the way to landing on a "correct" or in-key note. But you don't always have to pass over them so quickly. You can land on a few and milk them if you want. In fact, the chromatic scale can be played anywhere depending on what you are playing against or even what you are not playing against and whether the notes "work" or not is only up to you and what your goals as a musician are and what your opinion is of how well you are accomplishing those goals. Depending upon your perspective and how you approach music in general, an abundance of chromatic scales may be right for incorporation into your guitar arsenal.

Concerning the length of time out of key notes are usually played reminds me of a story about the guitarist, Jake E Lee. He had a solo on one of his *Badlands* albums in which he opened with an F octave played in 8th position against an E minor background riff. He held this octave for a long time and it sounded very out of tune. But I liked how it sounded. In an interview, Lee said he had a huge argument with his producer and had to fight viciously with the record company to keep that F against E opening to his solo. But he won in the end. Victory. Also, the avant-garde saxophonist Ornette Coleman made his entire musical career out of constantly playing "wrong" or "in-between" notes instead of so-called correct ones.

So if you want to twist up a few ear canals, you can incorporate the chromatic scale into your playing and use it every chance you get.

Now I will end with a simple lick that combines traditional blues phrases and the chromatic scale.

```
                        ~                                   ~
|------------------10------|-10-9-8---------------------|
|----8---8-10b12=====10r8-|--------10-9-8---------------|
|-/9---9------------------|----------------9-8-7b8------|
|-------------------------|-----------------------7-5-7-|
|-------------------------|-----------------------------|
|-------------------------|-----------------------------|
```

How to Become a Guitar Player from Hell

```
                                      ~                                      ~
|----------------------------------------5b6-5b6-----------|
|------------------------------------5h6h7---------8-5--------|
|------------5h7------------5h6h7-------------------7-5-6--|
|---------5h7----------5h6h7-----------------------------------|
|-----5h7--------5h6h7-----------------------------------------|
|-5h8-----------------------------------------------------------|
```

Notice the '===' line which means you are to hold the 10th fret bend as you play the 10th fret above it on the high E string. Also note that the strict chromatic scale is not used above, only chromatic behavior is exhibited in two places between the normal notes of the A minor pentatonic scale.

Palm Muting

Many interesting effects and sounds can be produced by muting strings with the palm of your picking hand. Keep in mind I am not talking about dampening strings to hamper any extraneous string noise from ringing out (although that is almost always necessary on a distorted guitar with high volume), but instead I'm referring to the act of playing the guitar while muting notes so that certain tones and effects can be generated.

Palm muting is done by pressing the fleshy part of your picking hand against the strings, with your picking hand positioned close to the bridge. If you play power chords on the lower strings with distortion while muting, it will produce a heavy, chunky guitar sound. But you can also use palm muting for playing on higher strings for certain sections of solos or for higher pitched melodic riffs.

One of the main things to remember when palm muting is not to let your hand get too far away from the bridge, that is, not allowing it to get too close to the fretboard, and also remember you want the flesh of your palm to faintly but securely touch the strings. If too much of your palm comes in contact with the strings, it will deaden them significantly and the notes will sound lifeless and blunted as if they have been suffocated with plastic or cardboard. You don't want your notes to sound dead or stifled.

This type of over-muting is actually a mistake I used to make in my own playing and eventually it was pointed out to me by one of my bass players. He said I was putting too much of my palm on the strings when I muted on heavy riffs, and that my picking hand was too far away from the bridge, and as a result the notes sounded toneless and dead. I was somewhat offended by his criticism at first, but then I decided to have an open mind and listen to him and change the way I muted my strings. He was correct after all and I moved my picking hand closer to the bridge and didn't press down so heavily and the tone of my palm-muted notes was much better and clearer and they rang out with more richness and body. Always strive for heavy chunky riffs but make sure there is some tone ringing out as well.

That is another important lesson in itself. Always be open to constructive criticism. Never close your mind to what someone is saying even if they are playing an instrument you have little respect for. (Only joking, I like the sound of bass guitars and there are some truly astounding and gifted bass players in the world.)

Now on to an exercise. Play the following riff with palm muting. First, practice it with your palm just faintly touching the strings near the bridge. Then play it with your palm pressed down harder and your picking hand positioned closer to the fretboard. Listen to the tonal variations produced when your picking hand is muting in many different positions over the strings and you are pressing downward with different degrees of force. Find the position that sounds best to you. Hopefully not too muted, you don't want to kill the tone, and not too light, you still want the muting effect to be heard. Discover the level of muting that sounds best to your ears. Now try this simple yet heavy riff:

```
     PM----------------------------|
    |----------------|----------------|
    |----------------|----------------|
    |----------------|----------------|
    |-2-0-2-2-2-0-2-2-|-----5-------4---|
    |-2-0-2-2-2-0-2-2-|---5---5---4---4-|
    |=0-0-0-0-0-0-0-0-|-3-------2-------|


     PM----------------------------|
    |----------------|----------------|
    |----------------|----------------|
    |----------------|----------------|
    |-2-0-2-2-2-0-2-2-|-----5-------4---|
    |-2-0-2-2-2-0-2-2-|---5---5---4---4-|
    |-0-0-0-0-0-0-0-0-|-3-------2-------|
```

Notice that in the first and third bars the E, A, and D strings are played open as a chord. You will want to make sure you can hear those notes clearly after playing and muting the E power chord. Try to get your muting level adjusted so that you can hear those changes in pitch clearly. The other chords are simply G and F# power chords arpeggiated.

Our second exercise involves playing on the higher strings and using palm muting. When muting on these strings you can't use the same picking hand position as for the lower strings. They take an even lighter touch since the lighter strings are easier to suffocate. You will have to experiment to find the sweet spot and get the perfect amount of tone ringing out. Change the position of your muting hand frequently in relation to your pickups while trying the following lick in C major, then listen closely to the overall tone as you mute with different levels of force.

```
       PM-------------------------------------|
|----------------------|----------------------|
|----------------------|----------------------|
|-12-10-9----10-9------|-9--------------------|
|---------12------12-10-|---12-10-9-10-12-10-9-|
|----------------------|----------------------|
|----------------------|----------------------|


       PM---------------------------------------|
|------------------------|----------------------|
|-13-12-10----12-10------|-10-------------------|
|----------12-------12-10-|----12-10-9-10-12-10-9-|
|------------------------|----------------------|
|------------------------|----------------------|
|------------------------|----------------------|


       PM----------------------------------------|
|-13-12-10----12-10------|-10--------------------|
|----------13-------13-12-|----13-12-10-12-13-12-10-|
|------------------------|-----------------------|
|------------------------|-----------------------|
|------------------------|-----------------------|
|------------------------|-----------------------|
```

When playing the highest sections of this lick on the B and E strings, you will have to lighten your muting considerably. Make sure the tone of the notes is still getting through but also strive for a crunchy muted effect.

Speed Picking

If you truly want to transform yourself into a guitar player from hell you are going to have to become adept at executing blazing speed picking runs. I don't mean tremolo picking, I mean having the ability to pick 32nd notes as you change from note to note in various scales. It is not easy to do cleanly and consistently. Yngwie Malmsteen and John McLaughlin and Al Di Meola are masters of this type of playing.

The only way to develop insane technique with speed picking is to practice executing every note of different types of scales as quickly as possible with the help of a metronome to build precision and speed. I definitely recommend purchasing a metronome and using it.

How to Become a Guitar Player from Hell

Before we go into some specific exercises, we need to discuss the different picking methods or styles available to us. There are two broad general categories that speed picking falls into, along with one type that may not be considered speed picking at all.

1) Alternate picking. Up, down, up, down, up, down... to infinity. No deviation from the pattern, your plectrum moving back and forth, the pick continuously moving in an up-and-down motion. With this type of picking you will never perform two consecutive down strokes or two consecutive up strokes, and most of the motion will come from the wrist. Many famous guitar players swear by alternate picking, so it must be effective.

2) Economy picking. There *can* be two consecutive down strokes or two consecutive up strokes with this method. Essentially, economy picking involves alternate picking but when changing from one string to another you can perform consecutive up or down strokes so the pick moves in the most efficient manner possible. If you finish with a down stroke when you are on one string and are going to the one below it, you will continue with another down stroke. This is the type of picking I use, although I never sat down and consciously told myself I was going to use economy picking, it was just the method that came most naturally to me when I would practice picking scales as fast as I could. Sweep picking also falls into the category of economy picking, I believe. Sweep picking is similar to a slow motion strum and is usually employed for playing fast arpeggios. With sweep picking, the pick simply moves up or down across the entire span of strings and if more than one note occurs on any one string in the arpeggio, those notes are simply hammered or pulled.

3) All wrist – a flamenco type of picking. This method probably shouldn't be included in this chapter, but I will list it here anyway since it is a type of picking I have seen. Mainly this method is used for tremolo picking and I have only witnessed Eddie Van Halen using it. He would arch his wrist over the strings with the pick clamped into his stationary fingers and then flick his wrist back and forth as quickly as possible while hitting only one string and keeping the rest from ringing out with his fretting hand. I don't think this type of picking could be used to play any scales precisely but it is a type of picking technique you should be aware of.

Some teachers say alternate picking will produce the most speed, while others say economy picking will. I believe it is simply a matter of taste as to which type you should use. My suggestion is to ultimately use the method of picking that comes most naturally to you. There was a point where I tried to practice strictly alternate picking because I thought it would help me play quicker and more precisely. But then I returned to economy picking since the alternate variety didn't seem natural to me. The last thing I want this book to do is churn out a bunch of robots or even a single robot, so you should try all types of picking methods to discover which one works best for you and stick with it. You may even invent your own type of picking method no one has ever thought of before. I hope so. As with all the techniques discussed in this book I want you to discover your own identity as a guitar player and truly fulfill your musical potential. Now on to an exercise.

```
A Mixolydian

|----------------------------5-7-9----|
|----------------------5-7-8----------|
|----------------4-6-7----------------|
|----------4-5-7----------------------|
|-----4-5-7---------------------------|
|-5-7---------------------------------|
```

Try the A mixolydian scale (or mode – more on modes in a later chapter) above using strictly alternate picking at first – down, up, down, up, down, ... then switch to economy picking – going from one string to the next in the most efficient manner possible. Whether you start with an up stroke or a down stroke for the economy picking is up to you, but with alternate picking you really should begin with a down stroke.

Now let's change to the D Dorian scale (or mode) and play it with economy picking first, then switch to strictly alternate picking.

```
D Dorian

|-------------------------------10-12-13----|
|-------------------------10-12-13----------|
|--------------------10-12------------------|
|--------------10-12-14---------------------|
|---------10-12-14--------------------------|
|-10-12-13----------------------------------|
```

Which picking method do prefer? Which type seems most natural to you? Go with the one that is instinctive and make it the main picking technique for your playing. But you might occasionally try to practice the harder method since it may help with your overall precision and articulation. It couldn't hurt. I don't think practicing an opposite method to the one you are naturally drawn to will confuse your motor skills any. Also practice the different types of picking using scales but not just running them strictly up and down from string to string, change the notes around and play many variations within the scale.

You can also try Eddie Van Halen's style of flamenco picking with the scales above, and if you do I am sure you will quickly realize it is only effective for tremolo picking notes, as it seems to me almost impossible to switch between strings cleanly with your wrist arched up above the body of your guitar while flicking the pick back and forth violently.

Vibrato

Vibrato is changing the pitch of a note in an undulating fashion to produce a vocal, singing-like quality. A guitar player's vibrato is extremely important to their overall style, there are many guitar players who have vibratos so distinctive they can simply "shake" one note and their name will immediately enter your mind. (Note that in this chapter I will not be discussing vibrato produced by a tremolo bar as that is an entirely different technique, here I am concerned only with finger vibrato.) Yngwie Malmsteen, the Swedish virtuoso, is a guitar player with an immediately recognizable vibrato technique – he usually plays with a wide, operatic style and in it you can hear his strong personality and confidence. Joe Satriani on the other hand has a quicker vibrato with a somewhat bizarre, science fiction feel to it. Stevie Ray Vaughan's vibrato is somewhere in the middle of those two ranges and totally packed with the soul of real blues.

The mechanics of good vibrato are relatively simple, but to develop your own style, to put your own "brand" on shaken notes, it will require many hours of practice and listening to how it sounds and also consciously thinking about what you are doing when you apply vibrato.

Let's start with a simple vibrato exercise using our index finger. The main thing to remember when shaking notes is that the movement should come from your wrist. First, play the G note on your B string at the 8th fret and apply vibrato as you hold the note and let the movement come from your wrist, pivoting it back and forth. Watch how the string moves as you are playing. You should be bending it upward slightly and then letting it fall back down. Keep your index finger in one position, lock it in place, and move your wrist upward and then down and the note will be shaken in the proper way.

Now change up the rate of the vibration.

Practice shaking the note quickly for awhile, with barely any upward motion.

Then practice applying vibrato slowly, trying to put a lot of soul into it.

Next, practice shaking the note extremely slowly, using an exaggeratedly WIDE vibrato.

Moving on, using your ring finger, play the F note on the G string at the 10th fret, and bend it upward so that the G note you played previously is the tone that sounds, then apply some vibrato. Try to make the vibrato of this bent note sound exactly as it would if you were playing it with the index finger on the 8th fret B string as you did before, similar to the "bend and check" method discussed in the Bending Strings chapter. Again, let the movement come from your wrist as you anchor your fingers into one position. Practice this bent note quickly, slowly, then WIDE, and try to come up with other variations after those.

If you feel like going a little "out there," you can try this vibrato exercise. It is sort of impossible to do, but attempting it may have some beneficial aspects. Think of a certain emotion: happiness, anger, jealousy, anxiety, joy, exuberance, hate, love, etc. and while you are practicing your vibrato try to convey those different emotions through the shaken notes. Yes, it is a little weird to attempt this but just think of it as an advanced exercise or "outside-the box" way of thinking that may improve your playing in the long run. You could try to play an evil sounding vibrato, then a soulful vibrato, a chaotic vibrato, any emotion at all, try to capture it with your wrist and fingers while shaking notes. (The subtler emotions won't be possible to convey, but you can still attempt them.)

On certain practice days it is a good idea to set aside 15 to 30 minutes to concentrate solely on practicing vibrato, shaking notes all over the fretboard in different speeds and styles. Don't forget to hit the extremely high notes near the 22nd fret and also the lower notes near the 1st fret.

When listening to new guitar players you weren't familiar with previously, pay attention to their vibrato and ask yourself if they have a type you would like to have yourself, ask what they could do to improve their vibrato, ask yourself if theirs is bland or exciting or if it adequately succeeds in capturing the particular emotion you think the guitarist is aiming for, or if it displays some aspect of the player's personality.

Another way to practice vibrato is to set your metronome to a moderate tempo, then go through one of your favorite scales, say the B Blues scale, and as you play, shake every note for one measure, using every finger of your fretting hand, even your pinky.

Another unusual technique is to apply vibrato by initially moving the finger up, away from the target note, then going back down toward the floor and bending the string past its original position so the string is going in different directions and the vibrato is produced as a result. This type is only possible on the middle strings and seems difficult to control. I have not practiced with this method extensively, but it is something you may want to explore.

Also, playing with NO VIBRATO AT ALL will convey a certain emotion or emotions. There are many jazz players who play without using any type of vibrato and in my opinion it is all right to go without it occasionally, but I would never be able to stop using vibrato entirely because I have too much soul.

How to Become a Guitar Player from Hell

On Rhythm Playing

In my early years of learning how to play the guitar I was not very interested in rhythm, I didn't practice it as much as I should have. Instead, I wanted to play solos. All the time. As I've already mentioned. Fast, highly technical, flashy and flamboyant solos at lightning speed, filled with insane technique and blistering virtuosity. I neglected a lot of rhythm playing because of this.

And I do not recommend that you follow in my footsteps.

Rhythm playing is very important and it can be an art form in itself – Jimi Hendrix was a great rhythm player who comes to mind (better at rhythm than soloing, in my opinion) and also Stevie Ray Vaughan. Jamming with a band or simply playing 'in the pocket' with a good drummer can be an awesome experience occasionally even more fulfilling than blasting out a masturbatory solo filled with every trick in the book.

For effective rhythm playing, you will need to have a good sense of rhythm. Most people already have natural senses of rhythm, while others do not. I have found that the more you focus on rhythm playing and listening to good bands, the more your sense of rhythm will blossom. If you do not have a good natural feel for rhythm, one thing I recommend is getting some early AC/DC records and learning a few songs by ear (most of them are quite simple and fun to play, full of mostly standard chords strummed in simple patterns), and play along with them as much as you can. Of course another band of your choice is possible but make sure they use equally simple grooves and easy chord progressions. (I will explain more about how to improve your sense of rhythm in another chapter.)

Rhythm playing won't be discussed very thoroughly in this book. One thing I will explain however is the importance of strumming and muting. When playing funk rhythms for example, it is important to let the movement of the strumming come from your wrist. Also, you should be able to mute all strings with your fretting hand and quickly transition into different chord shapes.

For practice, mute all your strings with your fretting hand and picking hand simultaneously, then simply generate a rhythmic pattern by strumming all six strings. This is known as "scratching" since you aren't sounding any real notes.

Tablature for scratching usually consists of listing a bunch of x's across the strings like this:

How to Become a Guitar Player from Hell

```
|-x-x-x--x-x-x--x-x-x--|
|-x-x-x--x-x-x--x-x-x--|
|-x-x-x--x-x-x--x-x-x--|
|-x-x-x--x-x-x--x-x-x--|
|-x-x-x--x-x-x--x-x-x--|
|-x-x-x--x-x-x--x-x-x--|
```

It is hard to denote rhythms with tablature, but basically we are just muting the strings and strumming them to generate percussive sounds. Once you have this type of rhythmic scratching down and can play it cleanly while muting and staying in time with the beat, start adding in partial chords while continuing to strum. Like this:

```
|-12-12-x-x-12-x-x-12-12-x-x-12--|
|-12-12-x-x-12-x-x-12-12-x-x-12--|
|-12-12-x-x-12-x-x-12-12-x-x-12--|
|--------------------------------|
|--------------------------------|
|--------------------------------|
```

This is simply a funk rhythm in E minor which you can end with a move up to F# minor like so:

```
|-14-14-14-14-14-14-14--|
|-14-14-14-14-14-14-14--|
|-14-14-14-14-14-14-14--|
|-----------------------|
|-----------------------|
|-----------------------|
```

Once you have that funk rhythm down, you can move on to another simple rhythm that uses an E7 flat 9th chord, and a D7 flat 9th chord, respectively.

```
   PM|       PM|        PM|       PM| ~
|-----------------|-----------------|
|-----8-8-----8-8-|-----8-8-----6---|
|-----7-7-----7-7-|-----7-7-----5---|
|-----6-6-----6-6-|-----6-6-----4---|
|-----7-7-----7-7-|-----7-7-----5---|
|-0-0-----0-0-----|-0-0-----0-0-----|
```

That is about all on rhythm guitar I am going to discuss in this book. But one more tip, pay strict attention to your sense of timing when you are playing rhythm. Don't speed up or slow down of get away from the beat and also try to be conscious of how your playing fits in with the drummer and the bass player.

Ultimately, as with everything else about the guitar, rhythm playing will take experimentation and hands-on experience and many hours of jamming and hopefully remembering what you played before that sounded good to you and then adapting it, increasing and modifying and building upon your rhythm knowledge to hopefully create your own style and then constantly working to add more things to your arsenal.

Taming the Fretboard With Modes

The fretboard is difficult to master. It contains a lot of notes. Many of them are the same, only in different positions of the neck – (you're probably already aware of this since (hopefully) you know how to tune your guitar using the 5th fret tuning method).

But we need to learn the fretboard. All guitar players from hell need to master the neck and be able to play in any position. It is a must. After playing for a few years and learning scales, chords, and arpeggios, you will soon be able to visualize many patterns and shapes on the neck that are instantly recognizable. You will see a lot of boxes and patterns that you can use in your playing whenever you merely glance at the neck. This is beneficial at first since you are just starting to grasp how the fretboard functions and how it can be broken down and organized into useful portions. But later on, when you get locked into this way of thinking and it begins to hamper your improvisations, you will have to break free from this simpler method and proceed out into the great beyond. Improvising solos or melodies demands that you have as much freedom of expression as possible. Knowing how to play the same lick in multiple positions is ultimately what you are aiming for, not having to use only one pattern in a particular portion of the neck. But now I am getting into a different lesson entirely and we need to take a few steps back.

Before we embark on a journey to truly master the fretboard, we need to first learn patterns and scales that will open up the territory for us, even if it is only in a primitive way. We will start by memorizing the key of C major in all positions on the fretboard. Doing this brings us into modal territory.

A mode is simply playing the notes of one scale in a different position of the neck and emphasizing a different tonic or root note along with other fundamental tones of the scale than the usual ones so that it produces a different "flavor" or "feel," even though we are still in the same key. For example, if I play the notes for C major but in the fifth position starting with the A on the low E string, I have just entered the Aeolian mode. Notice that even though I am still playing in C major, I can emphasize the A, E, and F notes of the scale in the fifth position and this will give me a different overall sound. A Aeolian will produce a "minor" sound and rightly so since A is the natural minor when we are in the key of C major. Also, the background chords will play a major part in determining the flavor of the melodies. That is the main idea behind modes, that you can play the same scale in any position of the neck, but if you emphasize certain tones in one portion the music will sound different.

How many modes are there? Only seven. Naturally, since that is how many tones there are in a major scale before it repeats with the root an octave higher. The names of the modes are Lydian, Ionian, Mixolydian, Dorian, Aeolian, Phrygian, and Locrian. The tonalities of the first three are considered "major," while the last four modes are considered "minor" in tonality. Now I will give you tablature for each of the modes with some explanation of each below. You should memorize these so you can begin your journey toward mastering the fretboard. Thinking of these as "scales" in different positions of the neck will probably make memorization easier, although there are a couple of mnemonic tricks you can use for recalling the names of the modes, which I will show you later.

```
          C Major Scale or C Ionian mode

|------------------------------------------10-12-13----|
|------------------------------------10-12-13----------|
|------------------------------9-10-12-----------------|
|------------------9-10-12-----------------------------|
|----------8-10-12-------------------------------------|
|-8-10-12----------------------------------------------|
```

The Ionian mode is just the major scale. To most people it provides a "happy" sound or a cheerful flavor. You should already know this one. (I have it listed in the 8th position here because I want the modes to span the entire fretboard. The positions I list for them will jump around quite a bit.)

```
              F Lydian

|-----------------------------1-3-5----|
|-----------------------1-3-5----------|
|-------------------2-4----------------|
|-------------2-3-5--------------------|
|-------2-3-5--------------------------|
|-1-3-5--------------------------------|
```

See how we switched to the first position? This is the Lydian mode. It starts with the F note and continues: G, A, B, C, D, E (as all notes of our modes here will, but beginning with different tonic notes!). Play this one starting with the first fret of the low E string. There are of course other positions, but remember we're trying to span the entire neck so you can properly memorize C all over the fretboard. Lydian is a major mode with a "happy" tonality similar to the Ionian. I hardly ever use the Lydian mode in my solos (not because it doesn't sound good or anything).

How to Become a Guitar Player from Hell

```
G Mixolydian

|----------------------------5-7-8----|
|------------------------5-6-8--------|
|--------------------4-5-7------------|
|--------------3-5-7------------------|
|--------3-5-7------------------------|
|-3-5-7-------------------------------|
```

The Mixolydian mode. Many rock songs and jazz songs employ this mode. It is considered to have a major tonality also, while some people (such as myself) consider it to have a bluesy feel as well.

```
D Dorian

|-------------------------------------10-12-13----|
|---------------------------------10-12-13--------|
|-----------------------------10-12---------------|
|-------------------10-12-14----------------------|
|-----------10-12-14------------------------------|
|-10-12-13----------------------------------------|
```

The Dorian mode. Our first minor mode so far. I frequently use this one with the minor pentatonic. I alternate between simple pentatonic box shapes and Dorian and also go into the blues scale. I like the Dorian mode. To me it has a minor bluesy feel. Notice with those mode we moved back to the 10th position. I prefer to always start my modes on the root note. That way I know where I am at all times

```
E Phrygian

|-------------------------------------12-13-15----|
|---------------------------------12-13-15--------|
|-----------------------------12-14---------------|
|-------------------12-14-15----------------------|
|-----------12-14-15------------------------------|
|-12-13-15----------------------------------------|
```

The phrygian mode. Many people consider this one to have a Spanish flavor. I think it sounds a tad classical, myself. I use this one a lot also. I prefer the minor sounding modes.

```
A Aeolian

|----------------------------5-7-8----|
|------------------------5-6-8--------|
|--------------------5-7--------------|
|--------------5-7-9------------------|
|--------5-7-8------------------------|
|-5-7-8-------------------------------|
```

41

Dropping back down to 5th position we get the A Aeolian mode, this is probably the most commonly used mode of all. It pops up constantly in heavy metal and rock songs. It is the natural minor of C major. A very nice mode. Extremely useful and thought provoking.

```
       B Locrian

   |---------------------------------7-8-10----|
   |----------------------------8-10-----------|
   |----------------------7-9-10---------------|
   |---------------7-9-10----------------------|
   |--------7-8-10-----------------------------|
   |-7-8-10------------------------------------|
```

The Locrian mode is by far the most unusual of the modes. It isn't considered major or minor, but diminished. I almost never use this mode in my improvisations, but considering how atypical it is and how exotic it sounds and that it is labeled 'diminished,' I should have incorporated Locrian into my playing long ago. I prefer exotic things. I like bizarre and perplexing sounds. It is a mystery to me why I avoided this mode for so long. Matter of fact, I am going to start exploring it much more in my playing from now on. That is one of the great things about music. Always something new to explore, always something unusual to delve into and trip out on and learn.

Again, the modes above are important for you to learn so you can properly visualize how the fretboard works in a certain key. Explore the different modes and get familiar with their tonalities and flavors and improvise with them. Memorize the modes in all positions (I think C major is the best key to begin with). Then once you have them memorized the fretboard will not be such a mystery. Also, move some of the modes up an octave on the fretboard and practice them in a higher location so you can have the entire fretboard covered and under your control (at least while you are working in C major, that is). You can then transpose the modes to other keys once you have C major down well.

By the way, do you need an easy way to remember the names of the seven modes? I can give you an acronym-based mnemonic (memorization aid) that is a sentence whose words begin with the same letter as the names of the seven modes. Are you ready? It might be a little scary. Here it is.

In Dark Places Lurk Many Angry Lions

Look at the first letter of each word above. See how they match the first letters of the modes listed below? Neat, isn't it.

How to Become a Guitar Player from Hell

Ionian
Dorian
Phrygian
Lydian
Mixolydian
Aeolian
Locrian

Modes will open up your playing dramatically. Study them, memorize them, absorb their sounds into your heart and soul, experiment with them and transcend the mundane. Make the modes your closest friends and also use them to astonish and banish your enemies.

String Dampening

Throughout this book I will often mention the phrase, "extraneous string noise" and you should know that I have not written it repeatedly just because I like the way that phrase sounds, which I do, the many syllables of the first word set up the entire group so that it rolls off the tongue and also the 'n' and 's' syllables go well together, notice that when considering those sounds in the phrase there is first an n sound followed by an s sound in the first word, then an s sound followed by an n sound in the second, then an n sound followed by an s sound in the third word. That is why the phrase sounds so nice to me, I believe. Not to mention the x sound which is unusual to find in any phrase. But the real reason I have mentioned "extraneous string noise" so much is that you do not want it in your playing and string dampening is very important for getting rid of it. The sound of a distorted guitar with high levels of gain is hard to control because the gain will amplify every little mistake and glitch in your playing. You want to play cleanly. Always very cleanly.

The word 'dampen' means to make dull or dead; to depress, stifle, or suffocate. Usually when you are dampening strings you are muting them with the extraneous flesh of your picking hand. There is that word extraneous again (I wonder if I used it correctly then). It is a nice word. But you should learn to dampen your strings as much as possible, I mean all of the strings that you are not wanting to sound out when you play.

I could try to go through every lick and phrase in this book and tell you precisely where to hold your picking hand and your fretting hand and how to hold your pick just right so that the non-played strings would refrain from ringing out, but it would take me a supremely long time and it would make this book about five times its current length (and I was hoping to keep this text as short as possible so as to provide the reader with only the essential "meat" of the various topics, only the very important pieces of information that you need to know to become a true guitar player from hell so you can do more jamming and wailing than reading.)

Dampening is important. There are a few different kinds and players call it different things. I have already discussed some of its aspects in the Palm Muting chapter. There is right hand dampening and left hand dampening. Right hand is performed by palm muting, mostly. Left hand dampening is when you release the pressure from the strings yet still keep contact with your fingers so they do not ring out, which is usually called "choking," I believe. There are so many types of dampening and they will each be necessary for playing as cleanly as possible.

When playing funk rhythms, for example, many players use both right and left hand dampening. This is called "scratching." The way it's done is you palm mute with your right hand (if you are right handed) and also lay your fretting hand over the strings with just enough pressure applied to mute them, then strum all six strings in sixteenth note or eighth note syncopated rhythms which produces a scratching sound.

But the scratching technique is not really what I mean to discuss when I talk of how important it is to dampen your strings. That is just one playing technique that uses dampening. In this chapter I am talking about how to play cleanly and by dampening here I am mainly concerned with playing melodies and keeping the other non-played strings from sounding out.

Gradually, over a few years, I found that when I would practice with a large amount of gain on my amplifier, which was usually most of the time, I learned subconsciously how to dampen the other non-played strings and I didn't even need to think about where my fingers were to play the licks, melodies, and difficult chords cleanly. So I believe if you practice enough and be slightly conscious of dampening the extraneous string noise then gradually you too will learn to control high amounts of gain over time.

Remember to always strive to play as cleanly as possible since a guitarist who has a bunch of garbage ringing out through their solos and rhythms will never be considered a true guitar player from hell.

Double Stops

Using the broadest definition possible, double stops are simply two notes played at once on the guitar. The notes can be any interval – you can even use open strings. But most often however, double stops are played by barring across two strings and striking those notes. Another way to think of double stops is that you are simply playing one note on a certain string, then

How to Become a Guitar Player from Hell

"doubling it" with another note on the string directly above or below your intended note to make a kind of harmony or add another "layer" to the note, if you will. (Double stops were originally used a lot in "skiffle" music, which is an obscure style of guitar music not performed much anymore.)

Here is an example of how to create double stops. Let's start by playing an easy phrase in A pentatonic minor:

```
                    ~
|-------------------|
|-------------------|
|-----5---5-7b9-7-5--|
|-5-7---7-----------|
|-------------------|
|-------------------|
```

A simple enough blues lick, right.

Now let's add some notes directly "below" the original lick by simply barring with the same fingers.

```
                    ~
|-------------------|
|-----5---5-7b9-7-5--|
|-5-7-5-7-5-7b9-7-5--|
|-5-7---7-----------|
|-------------------|
|-------------------|
```

The bend with two strings may be a little tricky, but overall it should be easy enough to execute.

Now let's try the same lick but this time we'll double the notes from below instead of above.

```
                     ~
|---------------------|
|---------------------|
|-----5---5-7b9-7-5----|
|-5-7-5-7-5-7b9-7-5----|
|-5-7---7-------------|
|---------------------|
```

So you can see how the original simple blues phrase was initially played and then we added other notes to create double stops to give it a different sound and feel. A very simple method for making easy licks sound fuller and perhaps more expressive.

The way I think of double stops on the guitar is that they are an easy technique for turning single note phrases into chord clusters by simply barring with the fingers. They are nice for adding more depth and character to your licks, or for putting another "dimension" into your playing.

For our last exercise, play this C# minor pentatonic scale normally, and then try it with every note "double-stopped."

```
    Regular
|-----------------------9-12-|
|--------------------9-12----|
|----------------9-11--------|
|-----------9-11-------------|
|------9-11------------------|
|-9-12-----------------------|

    Double Stopped
|--------------------9-12----|
|----------------9-11-9-12---|
|-----------9-11-9-11--------|
|------9-11-9-11-------------|
|-9-12-9-11------------------|
|-9-12-----------------------|
```

Because they have a bluesy sound, double stops work quite well when coupled with pentatonics and normal blues licks. Also, practice using hammer-ons and pull-offs with them too, and if you are feeling especially adventurous, you could attempt finger tapping double stops using the index and middle fingers of your picking hand and barring with your other hand for the hammer-ons and pull-offs!

Arpeggios

An arpeggio is simply the notes of a chord played individually or separately instead of all at once with the notes ringing out and blending together. So to play an arpeggio we could simply finger a regular C chord in standard position like so

```
   x 3 2 0 1 0
```

and pick each note in an up-and-down motion like this

```
|---------0------------|
|-------1---1----------|
|-----0-------0--------|
|---2-----------2------|
|-3---------------3----|
|----------------------|
```

How to Become a Guitar Player from Hell

But come on, this is not how a true guitar player from hell would play arpeggios. We need to execute more interesting shapes higher up the neck and put in some fast ass-kicking sweep picking into the mix so we get that genuine flash-trash into our playing (J. K.).

The shapes we will be executing in higher positions will also be based on standard chord or barre chord shapes, except other notes will be added in to get different chord voicings. The main thing to keep in mind about these arpeggios is they are very similar to barre chords you already know and thus can be shifted around the neck like barre chords to get different root notes.

The arpeggios I will soon list should be played using a technique called sweep picking (which I have already discussed in the Speed Picking chapter). Sweep picking is a method of picking that can be thought of as a slow-motion strum, whereby the plectrum "sweeps" across the strings as the fingers move and roll to grab the necessary notes of a chord. With enough practice, arpeggios can be played blindingly fast using sweep picking. If there happens to be two notes played on a single string in the arpeggio, they are usually hammered or pulled so as not to interrupt the smooth up and down motion of your plectrum.

(A brief aside here that may help you: when I was in a certain band my very critical bass player who I mentioned in an earlier chapter once commented that I was playing my arpeggios too slowly. He thought I wasn't sweep picking with enough speed. After careful consideration of his comments I realized that he was correct and I modified my performance accordingly. But the reason I was initially playing my sweep picked arpeggios too slowly is that I had heard on many occasions other guitarists execute arpeggios with sweep picking in a very sloppy way: they had a tendency to play the first couple of notes of the arpeggio cleanly and precisely, and also the last two notes with articulation, but in the middle they would roll their fingers and blur the pick down the strings and smear the notes and it would sound like an incoherent mess. You couldn't actually discern any of the pitches or overall tonality of the arpeggio. It sounded like a mish-mash of blurred clicks instead of notes. What good is that. They could have been merely muting the strings and scratching their pick against dead muted notes since there was no real articulation present. So to counteract this sloppy mush of garbage sweep picking, I went in the opposite direction and slowed down my sweep picking so much it sounded simplistic and ridiculous and I am glad my bass player had the sense to point out what I was doing wrong.)

When playing through the arpeggios below, keep in mind that although in the end you want them to sound fast and impressive, you also want to articulate every note and not have them merely be slop-fests with no tonality. (You can also forego sweep picking and add different rhythms to the phrasing

How to Become a Guitar Player from Hell

of your arpeggios, for example, the first three notes played in a triplet rhythm, then the second set of notes in a quintuplet pattern, etc.)

We will start off with a simple minor barre chord shape for our first arpeggio. Notice that the root note will be wherever our index finger happens to land on the 6th string. Here is an E minor arpeggio:

```
|--------------------12-15-12--------------------|
|-----------------12----------12-----------------|
|--------------12----------------12--------------|
|-----------14----------------------14-----------|
|--------14----------------------------14--------|
|-12-15----------------------------------15-12-|
```

The G note after the E on the lowest string can be hammered-on if that feels more natural to you. That is how most players perform it so they don't have to stop the downward motion of their plectrum to execute an up stroke. Notice that the notes on the 14th frets and the bottom 12th frets are barred and rolled (applying pressure on the picked notes only when the plectrum comes in contact) with the ring and index fingers respectively. Barring and rolling your digits cleanly is one of the keys to good sweep picking.

Next we will move on to a Maj7 shape. Again, wherever our index finger happens to be, that is the root note of this Maj7 arpeggio, even though we have now switched to the A string instead of the low E as above. So since we are playing this one starting with the 10th fret on the A, it will be a Gmaj7 arpeggio:

```
|----------------10-14-10----|
|-------------12-------------|
|----------12----------------|
|-------12-------------------|
|-10-14----------------------|
|----------------------------|
```

Play the arpeggio descending by following the same pattern. For the notes on the 12th fret, they can be played with the middle finger rolling across the middle strings at that position. Remember not to simply "mush" through them, but strive to articulate every pitch clearly and succinctly.

Remember what I said about the root note earlier? We can move the same Maj7 shape above down to the 5th fret on the A string so that it becomes a Dmaj7 arpeggio, like so:

```
|-----------5-9-5----|
|---------7----------|
|-------7------------|
|-----7--------------|
|-5-9----------------|
|--------------------|
```

How to Become a Guitar Player from Hell

Now we will move on to one of my absolute favorite arpeggios. It consists of a G major chord's notes but with an extension to higher notes in the same scale further up the neck.

```
|----------------7-10-7---------------|
|------------8--------8---------------|
|--------4-7------------7-4-----------|
|------5--------------------5---------|
|----5------------------------5-------|
|-3-7---------------------------7-3--|
```

I love this arpeggio. I regularly move it to the A position, the B position and the D position. But it will sound phenomenal anywhere. In the middle of this arpeggio, when transitioning from the 4th to the 7th fret, it will be necessary to slide up and change hand positions (which is something we have not done yet), but I find that the notes of this arpeggio fall quite naturally under the fingers even with the shift and it is very pleasureable to play.

Next is a more unusual arpeggio and one that sounds exotic since it incorporates a semitone (half step) interval. This is one I'm very fond of and I like to play it at gigs. I execute this one regularly in solos and usually add in some C# Phrygian phrases before or after it which sound quite nice. This arpeggio basically has the tones of an Emin13th chord, although I am not positive it strictly falls into that category. I am not confident about the actual theory underlying this arpeggio, but if any readers happen to know, they are welcome to contact me, (see my Bio at the end of this book for contact information).

```
|-9-10-9-----------------------------9-10-9----|
|--------10-------------------------10---------|
|----------11-------------------11-------------|
|------------12-9---------9-12-----------------|
|----------------10----10----------------------|
|------------------12--------------------------|
```

Again, I have not included hammer-on or pull-off instructions above because I want the tablature to look clean and tidy and also if you do not feel like hammering or pulling any particular notes you can of course pick each one if that is more comfortable for you. Remember you are aiming for speed, clarity, and precision here and in the end you should use whatever works best for your fingers, mind, hands, and heart and for keeping your soul vivacious.

Here are two more common types of barre chord arpeggios that you can use along the A string, changing root notes accordingly. Play them in all areas of the fretboard. They are easier to play in the higher register where the notes are closer together and fall easier under the fingers. These shapes are perfect for moving around and if you get your rolling and sweeping picking in perfect synchronicity you can generate a mind-boggling amount of speed.

```
A arpeggio

|------------------12-17-12-----------------|
|-------------14----------14----------------|
|----------14----------------14-------------|
|-------14----------------------14----------|
|-12-16-----------------------------16-12---|
|-------------------------------------------|


A minor arpeggio

|------------------12-17-12-------------------|
|-------------13----------13------------------|
|----------14----------------14---------------|
|-------14----------------------14------------|
|-12-15-----------------------------15-12-----|
|---------------------------------------------|
```

Now I would like to close this chapter by demonstrating how to develop your own arpeggios using different chord voicings than usual. I will show you how to work out the notes of an arpeggio for a particular chord that you are fond of.

Think of a chord you would like to create an arpeggio for. I have always loved the sound of suspended second chords. So let's generate an A suspended second arpeggio. Here is the chord:

```
   Asus2
X  0  2  2  0  0
```

First, write down the successive notes that occur in the chord. A, E, A, B, E. Now we need to work out some good positions for how those notes can fall on the fretboard that will be relatively easy to play in arpeggio form. Let's start with an A in the 12th position on the A string. Easy enough. Now we need a B note, so how about playing the 14th fret one whole step up from our A. That is about the best way it can be played. Now we can simply follow the barre chord shape and play the next E and A notes by hitting the 14th frets on the D and G strings, then continuing with the original Asus2 shape we barre the 12th fret notes on the B and E strings, then end by grabbing another A note on the 17th fret.

Here is how our arpeggio looks in the end:

```
|------------------12-17-12-------------------|
|--------------12-----------12----------------|
|----------14------------------14-------------|
|-------14---------------------------14-------|
|-12-14------------------------------14-12----|
|---------------------------------------------|
```

Notice the B note is the only note that provides the arpeggio with its sus2 tonality. Also, it isn't too difficult to play. I use my index finger for all notes on the 12th frets, then my middle finger to roll across the 14th frets and my pinky to grab the highest note on the 17th fret.

So you can see it is fairly straightforward to create your own arpeggios from chord forms you are familiar with and that you like. With other more sophisticated chord voicings, remember to move the notes around and reposition them so they fall easily under the fingers. Also move the Asus2 arpeggio shape above to other areas of the fretboard and practice it in many positions.

Legato Playing

Legato is an Italian word meaning "smooth," although its literal translation is "tied together." Legato licks and phrases are played so that one note flows into the next with no pauses, silences, or interruptions in between. The electric guitar is an easy instrument to play legato phrases on if you build up enough hand and finger strength and also utilize enough gain on your amplifier to enhance the articulation of the necessary hammer-ons and pull-offs. With enough practice, legato notes can sound just as loud and bright as picked notes. Many guitar players use legato to simulate other musical instruments, such as a saxophone, flute, oboe, trumpet, or other common wind instrument.

The basics of legato playing are hammer-ons and pull-offs. A hammer-on (as I'm sure most of you know) is simply pressing down hard enough on a fret to sound the note without having to pick the string. A pull-off is releasing a fretted note to one lower in pitch with enough force to sound the lower note. Simple. The goal with legato playing is to get the non-picked notes to sound as clean and smooth as possible while maintaining good consistency of volume throughout the phrase.

The main advantage to legato playing is that since each note does not have to be picked, a player's speed is enhanced considerably. (Although speed is definitely not the most important aspect of guitar playing, it is nice to have the ability to play quickly if the music or the player's emotions call for it.) Another advantage with legato playing is that many people find the smoother sound to be more natural, fluid, and appealing.

How to Become a Guitar Player from Hell

Let's start off with a simple warm up lick you can play as many times as you like to loosen up and stretch your fingers and hands. Try to play it consistently with each note sounding at the same volume.

```
|------------------------------------------------|
|------------------------------------------------|
|-11h12h14p12p11-11h12h14p12p11-11h12h14p12p11---|
|------------------------------------------------|
|------------------------------------------------|
|------------------------------------------------|
```

With this basic lick you only need to pick the first note while the rest are hammered and pulled. Make sure to mute the other strings and eliminate any extraneous string noise. Execute the hammers and pulls with precision and force.

Once you have played the warmup lick for a few repetitions, try shifting your hand around and playing other patterns using the same phrasing. Also you could try picking different starting notes of the phrase while still hammering and pulling the following three notes. Experiment with different groupings and find which combination or variation works for you. Use your metronome and try to increase the tempo gradually. Keep your technique fast and clean and think: "smooth, legato, ...
        smooth, tied together, ...
            smooth, legato, ...
                smooth, tied together, ..."

Now we will move on to a more advanced legato lick that is close (but not exact) to some of the phrases Joe Satriani likes to play.

```
|-------------------------------------------------|
|-------------------------------------------------|
|-4h5h7p5p4s5h7h9p7p5s4h5h7p5p4s5h7h9p7p5----|
|-------------------------------------------------|
|-------------------------------------------------|
|-------------------------------------------------|
```

The tablature is somewhat hard to read, but basically we have a 1-2-4 finger pattern sliding back and forth to fret two different scalar shapes. Only the first note of this lick should be picked while the first, second, and fourth fingers take over and use hammer-ons and pull-offs to perform everything else. Notice when switching positions from 4th to the 5th fret you slide your index finger up and maintain the 1, 2, 4, finger combination but employ a wider stretch between the index and middle fingers. I find that fingering to be the most effective. Practice this lick a lot, changing the speed of your metronome gradually. This one will greatly develop your hand strength and

How to Become a Guitar Player from Hell

finger muscles. Your hand will get sore if it is played long enough, but the improved speed and accuracy that results will be worth the pain.

Another legato technique I love to use live is one which involves muting. Now, legato and muting may seem like a strange combination, but they actually work quite well together. Check out the unique sound of this lick.

```
     PM-----------------------------------------------|
|---------------------------------------------------|
|---------------------------------------------------|
|---------------------------------------------------|
|---------------------------------------------------|
|-0h2h3h5p3p2p0h2h3h5p3p2p0h2h3h5p3p2p0h2h3h5p3p2p0----|
|---------------------------------------------------|
```

Begin by playing this one with no muting at all, just let the legato notes roll forth, then gradually apply pressure with the meat of your palm, being careful not to mute the notes too much, you don't want to completely deaden them, and continue with your hammer-ons and pull-offs. Even though we are using legato here, there is an added staccato (short and choppy) effect produced from the muting. Because we are performing this lick on the lower frets of the A string, they are lower in pitch and hence will ring out more. The lower notes add to the "chunky" rhythmic effect that is produced.

You may also like to try a variation on this legato lick. Simply start off in the same way, but after a few rolls on the A string, shift up to the D string and execute the same pattern, still muting with your palm. Move back and forth between the A and D strings while hammering and pulling the same set of notes and listen to how marvelous it sounds.

Scales can also be played with legato phrasing, usually just by picking the first note and hammering or pulling the other two notes on the same string, then you can shift your hand up the scale. On a personal note, I love using the legato technique for scales, but when I use it sometimes I actually feel guilty about not picking every note, thinking I'm almost "cheating" in a way since it is so easy to play scales in this manner. Here is a lick utilizing legato triplets in the key of A minor (or C major):

```
|-------------------|-------------------|
|-------------------|-------------------|
|-------------------|-------------------|
|------------3h5h7-|------------5h7h9---|
|-------3h5h7------|-------5h7h8--------|
|-3h5h7------------|-5h7h8--------------|

|----------------------|--------------------------|
|----------------------|--------------------------|
|----------------------|--------------------------|
|-----------------8h10h12-|------------------12h14h15--|
|---------8h10h12---------|---------12h14h15----------|
|-8h10h12-----------------|-12h13h15------------------|
```

```
|-------------------13h15h17-13h15h17-|-15--|
|----------13h15h17-------------------|-----|
|-12h14h16----------------------------|-----|
|-------------------------------------|-----|
|-------------------------------------|-----|
|-------------------------------------|-----|
```

Play the ascending triplets above as fast as possible but strive to retain the triplet feel.

The legato licks above should get you started shredding your way up and down the fretboard and your fingers will move so fast they may resemble the legs of a swift mongoose running from a tasmanian devil. Strive to develop different combinations and patterns and write your own legato licks and melodies.

Also check out some great players who frequently use legato techniques, such as Steve Vai, Joe Satriani, and definitely Allan Holdsworth who has a truly insane level of legato ability.

Natural Harmonics

Harmonics played on open strings are usually called "natural" harmonics to set them apart from "artificial" ones, which are commonly performed with the plectrum and thumb and also called "pinched" harmonics (more on that type later). Some people say *all notes* produced on a guitar are harmonics, and contain other harmonics too subtle to hear, and this may be true, but we are not going to delve into the scientific reasoning behind frequencies of string vibrations and the resulting sound waves produced that can trigger the doppler effect and also be divided into various points to create nodes where authentic harmonic points are located that are luscious and ripe for the plucking. Instead, I am going to make things easy, I am simply going to explain how you can play various types of harmonics on your guitar. How about that. And even though there are many names and ways to play harmonics on an electric guitar, in this book we are only going to be concerned with the two most basic types for the rock player: natural and artificial (again, the latter of which is sometimes referred to as "pinched").

Natural harmonics can be quite beautiful, they can add an effervescent and ethereal quality to your playing. To execute them, pick up your guitar and place your finger gently over the 4th fret on the G string and pick the note. Do not press the string down so that it hits the fret. Just lightly touch the string with your finger and pluck the note and raise your finger up. You should hear a high tone ring out. If you do not, try the procedure again, only this time move your finger a little closer to the fret, placing it directly over the fret if you have to, or move it around until you can hear the "sweet" spot where the harmonic note is located. Pick it again and this time if it rings out you have just played a natural harmonic and that is all there is to it, they are fairly easy to play once you adjust to the fact that they are not executed as normal fretted notes are. (Note: I have witnessed a few guitar players using natural harmonics to tune their guitars, but I never liked this method since I didn't think it was accurate enough – the regular 5th fret tuning method is good enough for me.)

The most important thing to remember with natural harmonics is where they can be played. As previously mentioned in a somewhat sarcastic fashion, there are certain points where the wave vibrations of a string are naturally divided up and it is only at these "nodes" that the natural harmonics will sound. Here are the necessary frets (memorize them) where harmonics are possible:

4th, 5th, 7th, 9th, 12th, 16th, 19th

The harmonics will sound across all strings at the frets listed above. (There is actually another harmonic just past the 3rd fret, but I didn't include it because it is fairly difficult to find the sweet spot there and bring it out, but it is there if you want to locate it and use it.) Note that the harmonics at the 16th and 19th frets sound exactly like those at the 9th and 7th frets, respectively. Also the harmonics above will only sound if you are using the standard tuning, but I assume you are using that for everything in this book.

For each harmonic you attempt on the frets listed above, practice getting them to sound by touching the string lightly above the designated area and then move your finger back and forth slightly while picking repeatedly to find the spot where the harmonic resides. It is usually directly on top of the fret or a little beyond it. This will also let you know if your guitar's "intonation" is off or not, intonation meaning that when your guitar is properly tuned, the notes in other places of the fretboard maintain their regular tuning and also retain their correct "frequencies" in relation to the other strings.

Usually the natural harmonics above are used in songs in the key of E, but other keys are possible. Since these harmonics can not be manipulated with the usual finger methods of vibrato and bending, tremolo bars are frequently employed to alter their pitch. The higher notes produced are most often used for bloodcurdling "screams" and such but you can also play mind-numbing "dive bombs" or pull the bar up and apply vibrato to simulate other harrowing and hypnotic effects. Edward Van Halen used natural harmonics quite a bit in many of his songs but he also loved artificial harmonics as well.

How to Become a Guitar Player from Hell

Below is a natural harmonic lick that might greatly improve your technique for the delicate nature of executing harmonics. The lick uses ringing open strings to provide contrast with the higher pitched harmonics, which creates a little drama, and drama in music is always fabulous. Also, play the lick faster toward the end, starting at the middle of the third bar.

```
|-------------------|----------------------|
|--------------<7>-|----------------------|
|--------------<7>-|---<4>-<5>------------|
|---<5>--------<7>-|-----------<4>-<5>----|
|-------<5>-<7>----|-------------------<5>-|
|-0----------------|-0--------------------|

|---------------------------------------------|
|--------<12>------<7>---------<5>---------<4>----|
|------------<12>-----<7>---------<5>-----<4>----|
|---<12>-----------------<7>--------<5>--------|
|-0-------------------------------------------|
|---------------------------------------------|
```

Notice that the harmonics are designated with less-than and greater-than algebraic symbols surrounding them: <x>.

String Skipping

Playing the same notes in the same scalar patterns can get old very fast. Imagine, a line of hundreds of guitar players all wearing yellow sequined uniforms, purple tassled hats and black combat boots, weilding maroon and black guitars with orange flamingos in flames, their fingers soaring up and down the fretboard picking the exact same notes of the C Major scale in the same mundane patterns. How crazy is that. A hideous depressing image that you do not want to be apart of. No way.

Although there are an unlimited number of ways to phrase and emphasize notes in any scale, during improvisations you may hit a brick wall and it may seem as though you are simply running the same patterns in the same boring combinations up and down the fretboard.

Do not worry. Many guitar players experience this problem.

I am going to give you the perfect solution to it.

It is called string skipping and it is a wonderful technique.

We'll break you out of that up and down scalar rut and add some wide intervals to your playing, which will thoroughly annihilate that rotten brick wall you have run into.

There are a few different ways to incorporate wide intervals into your playing (we will meet many in this book – tapping, open strings, arpeggios)

How to Become a Guitar Player from Hell

but now we are going to use a wide interval technique that uses a modicum of lateral movement. String skipping. If you are good with your picking hand, this shouldn't be that difficult. I have always been better at string skipping than I have at other techniques. It can be challenging to get the finger shifts down when skipping over entire strings, but they are also quite fun to practice at the same time. You have to get your picking hand and fingers coordinated for the licks to sound clean. Also you should use straight alternate picking on each of these riffs, up-down, up-down, up-down, ...

We'll start off our string skipping practice with a simple B minor arpeggio pattern:

```
|--------------------------------|
|--------------------------------|
|------6----------6----------6---|
|--------------------------------|
|---5-9---9-5---5-9---9-5---5-9--|
|-7----------7----------7--------|
  2 1 4 1 4 1 2 1 4 1 4 1 2 1 4 1
```

Notice I have included fingering information below the lick. 1 – index, 2 – middle, 3 – ring, 4 – pinky. Is this the first time I have included it? No. The reason I have is to show that your index finger should be used for playing the 6th fret on the G string as well as the 5th fret on the A string, which may not be obvious. That particular transition feels correct to me and I believe provides more accuracy.

Once you have the string skipping pattern above down smoothly, move on to this simple scalar run in A major:

```
|--------------------|------------------------|
|--------------------|------------------------|
|--------------------|----------6-7-9-7-6-----|
|----------6-7-9-7-6-|------------------------|
|--------------------|-9-7-5-7-9--------------|
|-9-7-5-7-9----------|------------------------|

|--------------------|----------7-9-10-9-7-9--|
|----------7-9-10-9-7|------------------------|
|--------------------|-9-7-6-7-9--------------|
|-9-7-6-7-9----------|------------------------|
|--------------------|------------------------|
|--------------------|------------------------|
```

Start off slowly, strive for clarity and smoothness, let your mind and fingers work together, use the Zen if you believe in it (just kidding – I'm saying that too much in this book).

Ready for some diversity in the string skipping department? The following lick changes things up from playing simple patterns and to me it has quite a distinctive classical flavor. It uses C major extensively with a couple of "accidental" notes here and there. Observe:

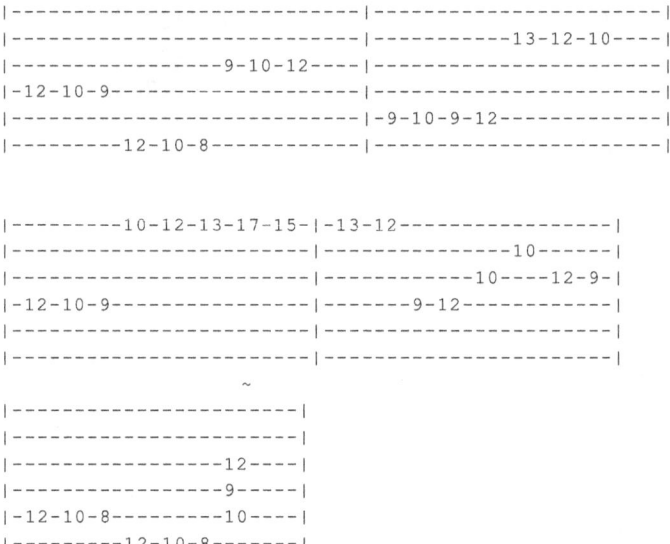

The last three notes are played simultaneously as a G major chord, and vibrato is applied to all three notes.

So there you have a few exercises to get you started string skipping toward oblivion and self-discovery and euphoria.

One other tip to remember: think about where your hand is going on the next string *before* you actually shift and play the notes. Let your mind jump ahead to anticipate where it is going next for the lick, so you will be prepared and can move your hand quicker to the new position and hence make the shift smoother between strings. If you visualize the next shift in this way you will make a better transition and the lick will be cleaner.

Another tip before I move on to the next topic (which is unrelated to this chapter): Never play your electric guitar while swimming in a pool or a pond.

Staccato Playing and String-Popping

Staccato is a nice but simple technique that you will probably not use frequently. Nevertheless it can be quite effective and will add some variety to your playing and can be very expressive if used tastefully. The word staccato literally means "detached" and it involves playing short and choppy notes on your guitar. To execute the technique one simply cuts off the notes shortly

How to Become a Guitar Player from Hell

after they have sounded – not letting them ring out – and then continues to the next note with brief moments of silence separating the tones. Think of it as the opposite of legato playing. During a solo, after you have played many bars of fluid licks with all the notes running together, you can suddenly change to staccato phrasing – short choppy notes – and it will sound exceedingly dramatic.

Practicing this style of playing is straightforward enough. Just play through some scales or licks and immediately stop the notes after they have sounded by releasing the string and allowing it to move up and away from the fretboard subtly while simultaneously muting the entire string with your picking hand. You will have to mute with both hands to keep down any extraneous string noise (as you know, with a distorted electric guitar this is almost always necessary).

Our first exercise will be to simply play the E phrygian scale (or mode) descending without letting any notes flow or bleed together. Perform it in different ways. First, play it soft and short and choppy without much emphasis, then play it loud and sharp but with short choppy notes (not breaking any of your strings), then try to determine which style you prefer. Here is a basic descending E Phrygian lick. First play it with eighth notes in staccato fashion, then play it in sixteenth notes normally with no staccato for contrast.

```
|-10-8-7------------|--------------------|----|
|--------10-8-7-----|--------------------|----|
|    -----------9-7-|--------------------|----|
|-------------------|-10-9-7-------------|----|
|-------------------|--------10-9-7------|----|
|-------------------|--------------10-8-|-7--|
```

Now we will continue with the E Phyrgian scale, except this time we'll start with a few notes using legato and vibrato (first bar), then transition into a staccato phrase for the ending (second bar) to make a stark contrast to how the lick began.

Try playing this one with sixteenth notes at the beginning and eighth notes at the end at about 140 beats per minute.

```
|-----------------------|
|-----------------------|
|-----------------------|
|-7--------------------7-|
|---7h9h10p9p7h9h10p9p7---|
|-----------------------|
```

How to Become a Guitar Player from Hell

```
                                         ~
|------------7-8-10-12-10-8-7-8-7--------|
|-----7-10-8----------------------8-7----|
|---9---------------------------------9--|
|-9--------------------------------------|
|----------------------------------------|
|----------------------------------------|
```

The quick hammer-ons and pull-offs at the beginning may be tricky, you can slow them down if necessary. After the vibratoed A note at the end of the first bar, begin the staccato portion by quickly sounding and cutting off each note, releasing the played string from the fretboard and using your picking hand to entirely mute the string from ringing out. You don't have to play strict eighth notes throughout the staccato section, you can vary the phrasing a little so that it slows down or speeds up, just make sure the majority of the notes stay short and choppy to produce the desired staccato effect.

Now on to string-popping. You may have already heard of this. It is another type of staccato technique which is not very well-known, or if it is well-known, it is not so popular that it's used frequently. I call it 'string-popping' although it may have other names. String-popping can be a somewhat 'over-the-top' or provocative technique that can sound quite impressive (and expressive) when coupled with the blues or minor pentatonic scales. Bass players use string-popping quite a bit, but they do so mainly for playing grooves and not while soloing. Actually, the only time I believe I have heard string-popping performed on guitar is on an old and somewhat obscure blue records by an individual whose name escapes me now, but I remember being very impressed by the sound since I had not heard anything like it before.

To begin popping strings, you have to learn how to pinch the strings with your fretting hand. Instead of picking the notes, we will use our index finger and thumb to pinch and pull the string upward slightly, then release it so that it snaps against the fretboard to produce a popping sound. The string will still vibrate in the normal way except a millisecond before it does you will hear it snap against the fretboard before it starts ringing. This of course produces a percussive effect similar to staccato. String-popping is under-utilized in contemporary music, but you should try to make it popular again. String popping. A neat technique.

Here is the lick to practice.
Pop each note instead of picking them.
Play it slowly and with feeling.

How to Become a Guitar Player from Hell

```
              ~              ~
|------------------8------|
|-------------5b6---------|
|-5-8-7-5-----------5----|
|---------7-5-------------|
|-------------------------|
|-------------------------|
```

Again, each note of the lick is sounded by the picking hand pinching the string, pulling it up a little, then letting it fall back to the fretboard. Notice the half step bend on the B string. Milk it. You can also put in more partial bends or smears on other notes to make the lick sound even bluesier.

You may be wondering what to do with your plectrum while you are busy pinching strings with your index finger and thumb. You will have to store it between the joints of your middle finger on your picking hand by cupping or cradling it there. Practice going back and forth between holding the pick normally between index and thumb, then laying it on your middle finger and curling it up so that it is cupped in the middle inside-portion of your second finger. With a little practice it will be fairly simple to move the pick back and forth. The pick fits well between most middle finger joints.

During a gig, make sure you keep plenty of extra picks handy in case you ever drop one. I usually pile a bunch of picks on top of my amplifier before gigs so I can quickly turn around and scoop one up if I lose the one I'm using.

Notice that the staccato effect produced by string-popping is not the normal method of cutting off notes, but instead the staccato sound comes from the string striking against the fretboard. It is still considered staccato because even though the notes ring out, the rhythmic snapping is vivid and conspicuous and terrifying enough that it produces a short rhythmic "note" of its own.

To generate even more staccatolike explosive sounds you can try popping double-stopped notes on the guitar. This is even wilder. Check it out. Get adventurous and experiment. Go crazy. Try to come up with your own ideas. Take string popping to places it has never been before and make it popular again. Use it all the time in your solos. Become a string-popping freak. Also try string-popping through entire scales and arpeggios, the more exotic the better.

You can incorporate string popping into your normal practice days by setting aside five or ten minutes here and there to play licks and solos using nothing but string-popping (but don't set your pick down anywhere, practice cupping it in your middle finger). Some people are of the opinion that when a player's fingers are in direct contact with the strings as they are when performing string-popping, it produces a more "earthy" or "gritty" or natural sound. I think I have to agree with them.

Developing Finger Strength

Strengthening your fingers will help you play with more precision and speed and dexterity, having stronger muscles in your hands and continuously working to build more power in your tendons will make a large difference in your overall playing. There are actually a couple of non-playing exercises you can do for strengthening your fretting hand which I will tell you about below. When I reveal the last exercise, you are probably going to think something similar to, oh that is easy anyone can do that, why is he giving us this exercise when it is so simple, this won't build much hand strength, but when you finally curl those digits around your well-worn fretboard and try the last set of exercises, you are going to know that it is not nearly as easy as it sounds and you might just say, oh now I see why, this exercise is pretty difficult after all.

Before we begin the hairy stuff, so we don't strain any muscles, we need to start off easy. Do this:

1. With your hand in the fifth position, place all four fingers on the 5th, 6th, 7th, and 8th frets of the neck.

2. While holding your third and fourth (ring and pinky) fingers down, raise the other two off the fretboard, hold them for a count of two, then set them down again. Repeat this ten times.

3. Do the same with the opposite fingers, that is, while holding your first and second (index and middle) fingers down, raise the other two up off the fretboard and hold for a two count, then set them down again. Repeat this variation ten times. You can think of this as trying to do hammer-ons and pull-offs if you want, with the fingers being set down with enough force to sound a note.

That is the easy warm-up. Now it will get more difficult. So get prepared. I hope your fretting hand is properly warmed up before you attempt this. Basically we are going to be doing the same exercise as above except now we'll use opposite fingers.

1. With your hand in fifth position, place all four fingers on the 5th, 6th, 7th, and 8th frets of the guitar.

2. While holding your first and third (index and ring) fingers down, raise the other two off the fretboard, hold them there for a second, then set them down again. It's harder than you thought, isn't it? Repeat this raising and setting down of opposite fingers ten times.

3. Do the same with your other fingers now, that is, while holding down your second and fourth (middle and pinky) fingers, raise the other two off the fretboard and set them down again. Repeat this ten times. Again you can imitate doing hammer-ons and pull-offs with the raised fingers.

How to Become a Guitar Player from Hell

Now we will move on to a chordal type of exercise using the same finger strengthing idea above, although the chords performed will be somewhat atonal and not great for the ears, but if played cleanly enough, they actually don't sound too bad. This exercise will be played exactly as the procedure outlined above, except now our fingers will span the first four strings of the guitar and open strings will be played when certain fingers are raised. Instead of describing this exercise in algorithmic form as above, I am going to list it in tablature form. Play it in eighth notes with a half note at the end of each bar.

```
|----------------|---------------|
|----------------|---------------|
|-6-0-6-0-6-0---|-6-6-6-6-6-6---|
|-5-0-5-0-5-0---|-5-5-5-5-5-5---|
|-4-4-4-4-4-4---|-0-4-0-4-0-4---|
|-3-3-3-3-3-3---|-0-3-0-3-0-3---|
```

Upon playing it you will see that the chords directly correspond with our first warm-up strengthening exercise above. Now we will move on to the more difficult version.

```
|----------------|---------------|
|----------------|---------------|
|-6-0-6-0-6-0---|-6-6-6-6-6-6---|
|-5-5-5-5-5-5---|-0-5-0-5-0-5---|
|-4-0-4-0-4-0---|-4-4-4-4-4-4---|
|-3-3-3-3-3-3---|-0-3-0-3-0-3---|
```

Getting the open strings to ring out cleanly will be quite a challenge and will require extensive practice, but work at it industriously and indefatigably, because this chordal version may strengthen your hands even more than the single string version. I am confident that one or the other will build up the muscles and tendons of your fretting hand until you can rip off solos better than Master Blaster can rip off a pig's head in Barter Town (Mad Max III: Beyond Thunderdome).

Once you have the above versions down fairly well, reverse the fingering so that your pinky is on the 6th fret of the low E string and play it that way. Also try it on other strings and in different positions.

If you practice these exercises enough, soon your digits will be crawling and wailing over your fretboard so furiously and passionately that during gigs the opposite sex will not be able to keep their hands off you. But your hands and forearms will be much stronger than theirs from performing the exercises above, so you will be able to fight them off easily, if that is what you desire.

How to Become a Guitar Player from Hell

Tremolo Picking and Miscellaneous

Similar to speed picking, tremolo picking (also called "double picking") is even simpler because with it you are not moving your fingers or switching strings to hit many different notes while rapidly picking with your plectrum. If you already have speed picking down fairly well then tremolo picking will be rather straightforward. All that is required is to pick one note as fast as possible on a single string. Of course you can change to other notes whenever you want, but to have it qualify as tremolo picking, I would guess you would have to pick any one note at least 10 or 20 times before switching to another. Tremolo picking is employed for a few reasons, mainly just for the speedy sound it produces, but also to sustain notes that would normally stop ringing out or that would not be heard clearly over other instruments.

Gypsy music and flamenco music regularly employs a lot of tremolo picking (mandolin players use it frequently also, but here I am speaking mainly of guitar music), it is an effect that turns up in many different styles, usually Latin in origin, but also Eastern European and American musicians use it as well. Bluegrass players tremolo pick many of their notes, and of course rock and metal players use it too.

The easiest tremolo picking exercise involves moving up or down a single string while following the notes of a particular scale. When using this technique, try to keep the volume and rhythm of all notes even, do not emphasize any one note over another. Here is a tremolo picking lick that uses A minor and moves up the B string and ends with rapid triplets (I hope your guitar has a 24th fret, if not, move it down to the 22nd fret).

```
|---------------|-------------|-------------|
|-3\\\-5\\\-6-8-|-10-12-13-15-|-17-18-20-22-|
|---------------|-------------|-------------|
|---------------|-------------|-------------|
|---------------|-------------|-------------|
|---------------|-------------|-------------|

|-----------------------------------------------------|
|-24-22-20-24-22-20-24-22-20-24-22-20-24-22-20-24-22-20-|
|-----------------------------------------------------|
|-----------------------------------------------------|
|-----------------------------------------------------|
|-----------------------------------------------------|
```

The first two notes have the '////' tremolo picking symbol while the rest do not. All notes in the first three bars are to be played in the same manner. The highest notes in the last measure should be executed as fast as possible and "crammed" together, cramming is where you really aren't concerned with

How to Become a Guitar Player from Hell

playing every note perfectly, but instead sort of flailing with control and "stuffing in" the notes as fast as possible.

Moving on, here is a tremolo picking exercise that involves the C minor pentatonic scale that changes from lower to higher strings, with a Dorian based run at the end.

```
|----------------------------------8-11-|
|---------------------------8-11--------|
|-----------------------8-10------------|
|------------------8-10-----------------|
|-----------8///-10---------------------|
|-8///-11///----------------------------|


                                              ~
|---------8h10h11---------8h10h11---------8h10h11s13--|
|-8h10h11---------8h10h11---------8h10h11------------|
|-----------------------------------------------------|
|-----------------------------------------------------|
|-----------------------------------------------------|
|-----------------------------------------------------|
```

Every note in the first measure is tremolo picked. Notice the slide at the very end of the second measure.

Another one of my favorite licks, but one that doesn't actually contain any bona fide tremolo picking is the following, which I love to play live since on many previous occasions it has almost sent certain audience members into a murderous frenzy. (Kidding.)

```
     PM-------------------------------------------------|
|-----------------------|-------------------------|
|-----------------------|-------------------------|
|-----------------------|-------------------------|
|-----------------------|-------------------------|
|-3-4-5-3-4-5-4-5-6-4-5-6-|-5-6-7-5-6-7-6-7-8-6-7-8---|
|-----------------------|-------------------------|


     PM-----------------------------------------------------|
|--------------------------|---------------------------|
|--------------------------|---------------------------|
|--------------------------|---------------------------|
|--------------------------|---------------------------|
|-7-8-9-7-8-9-8-9-10-8-9-10--|-9-10-11-9-10-11-10-11-12-10-11-|
|--------------------------|---------------------------|
```

This lick takes a bit of explaining. Even though I have tabulated it as if you are playing the notes in a 1-2-3 finger pattern and shifting positions up the neck, which is correct, your true goal with this lick is to play it as fast as humanly possible while moving your fingers and shifting but not really worrying about hitting *every single note* perfectly. This is how it is similar to tremolo picking, in my mind. You are going to be muting with your fretting hand as you pick rapidly and move your fingers up the neck, but you should really be "cramming" the notes in while playing and not caring about the execution of every single pitch. The muting and chromatics will take over most of what you hear when you play it superfast so any "mistakes" won't be audible and the lick will achieve its tension-building effect. At the end, when you get up to around say the 12th fret and are still on the A string, you can go into an A minor scale and play melodically again to get yourself out of the chromatic pattern and open it up to real music. Here is one way the lick could end:

Tremolo picking is quite fun and in spite of being rather simple once you have mastered the more general technique of speed picking it can add some spice and a different sound to your playing. Don't underestimate the easier techniques for producing interesting, exhilarating, and compelling sounds.

One and Two-Handed Tapping

Although he did not invent the technique, Edward Van Halen greatly popularized two-handed tapping by using it extensively in his solos (a guitarist by the name of Jimmie Webster was probably the first to make records in which he featured the finger tapping technique – although it is thought that the virtuoso violinist Paganini also used some form of tapping on his violin in the 1800s!). By "tapping" I am referring to the technique whereby fingers of the fretting hand are used to reach up and fret notes (execute hammer-ons and pull-offs) directly on the fretboard itself, which produces a distinctive legato sound. I am sure most readers of this book are familiar with finger-tapping or one and two-handed tapping – some inexperienced guitar players try it when

How to Become a Guitar Player from Hell

they first pick up a guitar (as I did) before they have learned anything else. One-handed tapping (a misnomer since both hands are actually used) is the use of one finger on the fretting hand to hammer notes on the fretboard, while two-handed tapping is the use of more than one finger on the fretting hand to sound notes.

    Certain aspects of tapping (such as repeating triplet patterns) have been overdone quite a bit over the last 30 years (wow! has it really been that long since Van Halen released their groundbreaking debut album and Eddie's "Eruption" blew other guitarists and musicians away? Yes it mocertainly has.) Still there is plenty of room for exploration and improvisation in the area of tapping if one incorporates different phrasing and uses more sophisticated scalar patterns. Tapping is a technique that is relatively easy to perform after only a small amount of practice, but there are a few things you will want to avoid when using it for solos, such as repeating triplets.

    In Eddie Van Halen's solo "Eruption," he performs a plethora of repeating arpeggio triplets that move their way up the neck. If you were to use these in a solo today, they would be instantly recognizable but in kind of a bad way. You would be using a phrasing method and style of playing that was fresh about 30 years ago, which isn't too good unless you are trying to pay an obvious tribute to Eddie's "Eruption."

    Nevertheless, triplets are good for getting the rudiments of tapping down, and they are fine when limited to your private practice room. Let's start off with a triplet based lick just to get the feel of two-handed tapping.

```
      T     T     T     T           T     T     T     T
|---------------------------|------------------------------|
|---------------------------|------------------------------|
|---------------------------|-11p4h7h11p4h7h11p4h7h11p4h7--|
|---------------------------|------------------------------|
|-10p3h7h10p3h7h10p3h7h10p3h7-|----------------------------|
|---------------------------|------------------------------|

      T     T     T     T           T     T     T     T
|---------------------------|------------------------------|
|---------------------------|--10p5h8h10p5h8h10p5h8h10p5h8--|
|---------------------------|------------------------------|
|-10p4h7h10p4h7h10p4h7h10p4h7-|----------------------------|
|---------------------------|------------------------------|
|---------------------------|------------------------------|

      T     T     T     T           T     T     T     T    T~
|---------------------------|-12p5h8h12p5h8h12p5h8h12p5h8-|
|---------------------------|------------------------------|
|-11p4h7h11p4h7h11p4h7h11p4h7-|----------------------------|
|---------------------------|------------------------------|
|---------------------------|------------------------------|
|---------------------------|------------------------------|
```

How to Become a Guitar Player from Hell

Notice the vibrato applied to the last note above. Holding the tapped high E note while applying vibrato with your fretting hand can be somewhat tricky, but it can have a charming and pleasant effect.

Once you have the feel of tapping triplets down (and it shouldn't take long) you can move on to other more interesting licks. Remember that when writing or composing your own tapping licks, you should use tapped notes as extensions of the scales you are working in (but that should be obvious at this point).

Here is a lick that uses the open E string as a pedal point (a regularly repeating tone in a phrase). This lick is rather hard to transcribe because it is not played in strict 16th notes, i.e. not all the notes are played with the same time duration. The ones that occur in the middle of the lick on the fretboard are "rushed" or "crammed" together, meaning they are played faster than the others. Still, I have transcribed it using standard 16th notes, even though that is not really how it should be performed. All I can say is that the tapped notes on the 12th fret are the ones emphasized, and when the open E string is sounded on the descent, that note too is emphasized, while the notes in between are crammed together.

I apologize for not being able to get the rhythms correct in the transcription for this lick.

```
                T                          T
|-5p0h5h7h8h12p8p7p5p0-|-5p0h5h7h8h12p8p7p5p0----|
|----------------------|-------------------------|
|----------------------|-------------------------|
|----------------------|-------------------------|
|----------------------|-------------------------|
|----------------------|-------------------------|


                 T                           T
|-7p0h7h8h10h12p10p8p7p0-|-7p0h7h8h10h12p10p8p7p0---|
|------------------------|--------------------------|
|------------------------|--------------------------|
|------------------------|--------------------------|
|------------------------|--------------------------|
|------------------------|--------------------------|
```

Bending strings and tapping different notes while holding the bend is another neat effect I use frequently in solos. I first saw Eddie Van Halen do this in his solo on the song "5150" which was the tune that initially inspired me to learn guitar in the first place. Here is a lick that uses the B minor pentatonic scale and bent notes with tapping further up the fretboard.

How to Become a Guitar Player from Hell

```
                          T       T      T      T
|-7b7.5-----------------------------------------|
|-------10-7------------------------------------|
|------------9b11r7-9b11=h14p9h12p9h14p9h16-----|
|------------9b11r7-----------------------------|
|-----------------------------------------------|
|-----------------------------------------------|


        T      T     T     T     T     T    ~       ~
|----------------------------------------|-------|
|----------------------------------------|-------|
|-9h17p9h16p9h14p9h19p9h17p9h14p9-7--|-[9]----|
|----------------------------------------|-------|
|----------------------------------------|-------|
|----------------------------------------|-------|
```

Yes, I realize the tablature for this lick is quite messy and a little confusing so I will explain the most important parts. It begins with a half step bend on the high B, then goes down the pentatonic and into a double stop bend. The G string is bent up a full step at the 9th fret and while holding that bend I use the index finger of my picking hand to fret the 14th fret on the bent G string, then pull off and tap on the 12th, 14th, 16th, 17th, and 19th frets, which are just extensions of the scale, alternating the taps back and forth on different notes, all the while continuing to hold the bend at the 9th fret, then finally releasing and hitting a pinched harmonic on the 9th fret G string (pinched harmonics are explained in the next chapter).

Tapping on bent strings sounds great. Usually I start off the tapped notes slowly and then gradually increase their tempo. You can bend and hold notes and apply vibrato, shaking them with your fretting hand to produce "wild" and outlandish effects.

Our final tapping example is similar to one I heard Yngwie Malmsteen perform on one of his albums (I forget which one), but the lick below is not exactly the same as his. You should play this tapping lick extremely fast, and if done accurately and with enough speed it will sound almost like the buzzing of a bumblebee. That is what it first reminded me of when I heard Yngwie play a lick similar to this one.

```
 T                 T                    T                 T
|-17p14h16p14p12h17p14h16p14p12h|-17p14h16p14p12h17p14h16p14p12--|
|-------------------------------|--------------------------------|
|-------------------------------|--------------------------------|
|-------------------------------|--------------------------------|
|-------------------------------|--------------------------------|
|-------------------------------|--------------------------------|
```

Each of the tapping licks above are pretty commonplace nowadays in the world of rock guitar. But tapping has been taken to entirely new levels in the last ten years or so with guitarists using more and more fingers to sound notes on the fretboard. Many guitarists use their index and middle fingers to perform tapped runs, but a few have incorporated all eight fingers into the mix and then tap all over their necks as if they are playing a piano. This is called "two-handed tapping" (see Stanley Jordan's tapped version of "Stairway to Heaven" which is truly incredible, the man is from another planet, you should be able to find the video on youtube.com) even though both hands are also used with one-handed tapping. As far as guitarists getting progressively more and more extreme with tapping techniques, it actually wouldn't surprise me if a guitarist soon popped up who had found a way to use even his thumbs on the fretboard, thus getting all ten fingers into the mix. But then only a year or so later we would hear of another guitar player who crawled out of the woodwork to use all ten fingers plus his tongue with a big scab on the end to play wickedly sick solos as fast as humanly possible so that the audience members couldn't even distinguish half the notes. And maybe at the end of his performance this new guitar hero would stick out his tongue after executing a long gruesome tapped run to reveal the thick half-inch long scab on the tip which he would wag back and forth and wiggle exaggeratedly for the pleasure of his captivated audience, and soon several women in the front row would go into a state of ecstasy and swoon. Only kidding, again.

 There are also guitar-like instruments designed exlusively for two-handed tapping methods, the "Chapman Stick" and "Mobius Megator" being two such examples.

 When tapping, you will have to make sure you mute all the strings you are not playing so they don't ring out. Extraneous string noise can be quite a problem, and one of the main things about learning to play guitar is how to control the strings you do not want to sound. Usually when tapping the palm of your tapping hand will lay across the unplayed strings and prevent them from ringing out, which reminds me of another tip concerning a method of finger tapping practice, which can be quite fun. Take a sock or a long piece of cloth and tie it around your fretboard near the nut so all the strings are dampened. Now you can set your plectrum down and concentrate solely on finger tapping without having to worry about any extraneous string noise bringing you down. Play tapped scales and improvise all over the fretboard, try out both your middle and index fingers for tapping and as many other fingers as you want. When you have quite a few runs mastered that are of an entirely different nature than the tapped licks you normally play, take off the piece of cloth or sock and try to play the new runs without the dampening behind them. The "sock dampening" technique may give you a new level of confidence and later you may be able to handle the extraneous guitar noise without the dampener on, after you have been practicing both with and without it for a while.

How to Become a Guitar Player from Hell

Also when fretting with your tapping hand, a slight flick (movement) of your tapping finger either up or down when pulling off can help "brighten" the pulled notes and increase the string vibration and hence the volume level.

When writing your own tapped licks, make sure you follow the notes in the scale you are working in, although it is also possible to incorporate dissonance and "outside" notes or chromatics when tapping, which are sometimes very effective.

Artificial or Pinched Harmonics

Artificial harmonics, in my opinion, are one of the main things separating the general dynamics of acoustic guitars from electric guitars (I am actually going to be showing you "pinched harmonics" in this chapter, but there are other types of artificial harmonics which I will mention in another chapter). Natural harmonics on an acoustic guitar ring out well, but artificial ones do not and are quite difficult to play on that instrument (at least for me anyway, perhaps a few readers can point out examples of acoustic guitarists who can perform artificial harmonics audibly, see my email address near the back of this book). The distortion and gain on an electric guitar are what make artificial harmonics possible. Plus pinched harmonics require a higher degree of subtlety and technique than natural harmonics.

So how does one play pinched harmonics? I would bet that half the people reading this book already know how to play them, since this text is not aimed at absolute beginners, but still I will explain them anyway.

Pinched harmonics can be quite demanding to perform well. To play them consistently you will need quite a bit of practice and also a precise picking hand technique. First, make sure the distortion level or gain on your amplifier is set rather high before attempting any pinched notes. Next, grab your guitar and play the following lick, which is in A minor pentatonic.

```
            ~              ~
|-------------------------------|
|-------------------------------|
|-7-5-[7]b9===5---5b5.5---------|
|---------------7------7-[5]----|
|-------------------------------|
|-------------------------------|
```

Note that the artificial harmonics are the ones with boxes around them. The third note is bent up a full step after the pinched harmonic has been performed and vibrato is then applied. But I haven't explained how to play pinched harmonics yet. Here goes.

Pick the string normally but as soon as you pick it, allow a tiny portion of the flesh of your thumb to come into contact with the string. This is what produces the harmonic. What should happen is that when you pick, a sort of "digging in" to the string will occur so that your thumb hits it a millisecond after the plectrum does and it causes a small harmonic to sound. You may need to move your fretting hand forward or back while practicing picking the note so that the flesh of your thumb finds the right "sweet" spot and the harmonic rings out. Position your hand in different ways near the bridge to get different harmonics. You will produce higher pitched harmonics the closer your hand is to the bridge, which are more difficult to bring out with clarity and volume.

Back to the lick above. The reason I play the two normal notes first is that they get the strings vibrating and sort of "set up" the artificial note that follows.

The key to pinched harmonics is consistency and the key to consistency is lots of practice and practicing the guitar is a hell of a lot of fun – it better be since that is the only way you are going to improve.

Practice playing harmonics by running through entire scales normally at first, then play them with artificial harmonics added to every note. And strive to develop subtlety in your picking hand.

Bizarre Almost-Uncontrollable Bends

Using strange, almost out-of-control sounding bends is another way to set yourself apart from the pack of similar-sounding guitarists out there. When you perform the following types of bends they will usually have a sitar-like quality or a sound that is oriental in nature. I believe I first encountered these types of bends from John McLaughlin who was very much inspired by Indian classical music, so much so that he formed a band called Shakti with a group of traditional or "classical" Indian musicians, which I have mentioned before in another chapter. They played wonderful and complex jazz-influenced yet traditional Indian-sounding songs made up of extended improvisational passages. And McLaughlin incorporated many wide interval bends that focused on microtones in his solos and the effects were unique, surprising, and seductive. One of the great things about executing these bizarre wide interval bends is that the sounds can often surprise even the person playing them.

Have a look at this lick which uses bizarre bends of a few different intervals:

```
|----------------------------------------------------|
|-(9tr12)10p9b[sharp half step bend and slow release]-|
|----------------------------------------------------|
|----------------------------------------------------|
|----------------------------------------------------|
|----------------------------------------------------|
```

How to Become a Guitar Player from Hell

The tabulature is in a slightly different form for this lick. The phrase above involves doing a trill on the B string by holding down your index finger on the 9th fret and hammering and pulling with your pinky finger on the 12th, then using your middle finger to grab the 10th fret, quickly picking the note there and pulling off to the 9th fret while yanking upward on the string and hitting a half-step bend, but then quickly releasing it to get various microtonal pitches in between – quarter and eighth step bends – and continue moving the string up and down, smearing it around. The more forcefully you perform the strange bends, the better they will sound. You can also go above a half-step into three-quarter and full-step bends. You want the bend to almost be uncontrollable sounding to produce an eerie effect. Try to imitate the sound of a sitar at first, then take it to places no other instrument has ever gone before. (You could even manipulate it simultaneously with your tremolo bar, although personally I don't use one.)

A suggestion for only the bends could be something like this:

```
|----------------------------------------------|
|-(9b(1/2)r(1/4)b(1step)r(1step)b(1 1/2steps)r--|
|----------------------------------------------|
|----------------------------------------------|
|----------------------------------------------|
|----------------------------------------------|
```

You could experiment with performing the bends with different fingers as well, and you could of course eliminate the trill at the beginning too, the important thing to focus on is the intervals of the bent notes (I find that using my index finger for the bend helps me hit the microtones easier, but you may want to use other fingers). Here is another suggested lick that again uses a trill:

```
|----------------------------------------------|
|-(9T16)9h10p9b~[tap with finger for trill]---|
|----------------------------------------------|
|----------------------------------------------|
|----------------------------------------------|
|----------------------------------------------|
```

In this version you tap with your middle or index finger of your picking hand to produce the beginning trill (usually you will be able to trill much faster this way) then release it to the 9th fret, hammer on with your middle finger on the 10th fret, pull off and start in with the uncontrollable yanking bends, using your index finger to try and hit as many abnormal tones as possible.

How to Become a Guitar Player from Hell

Extreme Lick #1 - Sweep Picking, Chromatics, Blues

To illustrate how many of the topics in this book can be combined to create your own musical phrases, I am going to list a few "extreme licks" that showcase different techniques used together. There will only be three Extreme Lick chapters but the melodies and phrases exhibited in them can be considered models and suggestions for you to build upon (although they are "complete" licks when played as written). Think of them as examples of ways that dissimilar phrases or techniques can be put together to exemplify a type of style or feel you want to capture in your playing, which you can then expand upon or twist and modify as you see fit.

    The extreme lick below demonstrates two different techniques: sweep picking arpeggios and the use of chromatic tones (and I have ended the lick with a few blues phrases in C# minor), which can have quite an eerie effect when used together. Again, the thing to remember when sweep picking is to never allow the "in-between" notes of the arpeggio to sound like mush or garbage. Many players will play the first and last notes clearly but then blur the middle notes of the arpeggio. Do not do that. Strive to articulate every tone. It is also recommended that you don't hammer or pull any notes below, so your picking technique will be improved as well.

    The flavor of this lick is classical from the arpeggios (simple Maj7th chord shapes ascending in whole steps) with a touch of "Flight of the Bumblebee" from the descending chromatics. The transition at the end into the blues phrases provides contrast and shakes things up a bit.

    Practice this with a metronome and gradually increase the tempo, always striving to play it as cleanly as possible.

```
|-----------3-5-7-9-8-7-6-8-7-6-5-|
|--------5------------------------|
|-------4-------------------------|
|-----5---------------------------|
|-3-7-----------------------------|
|---------------------------------|


|-----------5-7-9-11-10-9-8-10-9-8-7--|
|---------7---------------------------|
|-------6-----------------------------|
|-----7-------------------------------|
|-5-9---------------------------------|
|-------------------------------------|
```

```
|------------7-9-11-13-12-11-10-12-11-10-9-|
|---------9--------------------------------|
|-------8----------------------------------|
|------9-----------------------------------|
|-7-11-------------------------------------|
|------------------------------------------|
                       ~                          ~     ~
|-----------------------9---------------------------------|
|-----------------------12-9b9.5--------------------------|
|-11b13r9-11b13r9-9-11b14------------12-11-9-12-11-9------|
|----------------------------------------------------9-11-|
|---------------------------------------------------------|
|---------------------------------------------------------|
```

The first three measures are relatively straightforward, they involve picking 16th notes in an even fashion, but the last measure is hard to transcribe. You don't have to play the notes exactly as they appear in the tablature (in fact, you shouldn't since it is not an especially interesting lick). What I usually do there is improvise for a full measure in C# minor pentatonic after playing the first three arpeggios and chromatic patterns.

Incorporating Open Strings

Open strings played along with fretted notes can add another dimension if you will to your solos and improvisations. Open strings are actually quite natural to work into your licks and relatively easy to play. They are also perfect for performing pull-offs and hammer-ons as long as you make sure to execute them cleanly. A great deal of speed can be generated using open strings in conjunction with hammer-ons and pull-offs and they are also handy for producing a pedal-point effect (remember, pedal point means a note that is repeated or sustained as other notes change in relation to it). Incorporating open strings into your solos will open up your playing in new ways.

To give you a few ideas of what can be done, I will explain a few of my favorite open string licks. The first one is in the key of E minor and I use it frequently with bluesy improvisations after I have grown tired of wailing around in E minor pentatonic or the E blues scale or any of its variations. Begin by rapidly picking the open high E string and doing pull-offs with notes from the E minor or E pentatonic scales. Shift your hand around and change things up, there is no need to maintain any specific pattern. Just try different notes as you feel them. The lick actually looks harder to play than it is. You can build a lot of speed with this one and it sounds impressive even though it is rather easy to execute.

How to Become a Guitar Player from Hell

```
|-3p0-0-0-0-5p0-0-0-0-|-3p0-0-0-0-7p0-0-0-0-|
|---------------------|---------------------|
|---------------------|---------------------|
|---------------------|---------------------|
|---------------------|---------------------|
|---------------------|---------------------|


|-5p0-0-0-0-10p0-0-0-0-|-7p0-0-0-0-8p0-0-0-0-|
|----------------------|---------------------|
|----------------------|---------------------|
|----------------------|---------------------|
|----------------------|---------------------|
|----------------------|---------------------|
```

    Here you are basically tremolo picking the open high E string and then "cramming" in the pull-offs with your index and middle finger as your hand shifts up and down the neck. The lick is extended beyond the four measures above, usually I play it for quite a while. It is a nice flashy lick since your fretting hand and fingers are moving rapidly around the neck shifting positions while the high open E continues to ring out. Try different things with this one. Use more exotic notes in relation to the high E. Switch to the B string, even though you will have to mute the high E with a finger of your picking hand (probably your middle finger layed against it), it is still easy to perform the pull-offs cleanly and efficiently on the other strings as long as proper muting is involved.

    Chromatic patterns and open strings can also build a lot of pleasant tension in your solos. Here is an open string lick that uses the same finger pattern throughout with multiple hammer-ons to create an escalating effect of sheer panic as your fingers crawl up the neck like the legs of a deadly brown recluse spider. The thing to remember here is not to play this lick for very long as the chromaticism can wear on the listener and bring down their spirits – only a few moments of chromatic patterns and open strings is enough to achieve the desired tension without sending your audience into frantic convulsions.

```
|---------------------|------------------------|
|---------------------|------------------------|
|-0-0-2h3h5-0-0-3h4h6-|-0-0-4h5h7-0-0-5h6h8----|
|---------------------|------------------------|
|---------------------|------------------------|
|---------------------|------------------------|

                                                        ~
|-----------------------|------------------------------------|
|-----------------------|------------------------------------|
|-0-0-6h7h9-0-0-7h8h10-|-0-0-8h9h11-0-0-9h10h12-0-0-14b16-|
|-----------------------|------------------------------------|
|-----------------------|------------------------------------|
|-----------------------|------------------------------------|
```

How to Become a Guitar Player from Hell

The hammer-on triplets work in nicely with the open string played twice. You can get your fingers into a good flow by simply picking and maintaining the same finger pattern and writhing your way upward. This lick is fun to play and also sounds tolerably weird.

Our last open string exercise is a little more challenging. It uses notes from the C major scale and a lot of position shifting as you descend. Also there is only one note played on the open string between the fretted ones so you will have to move your hands and fingers quickly. All the notes are pulled-off to the open strings but I didn't include that in the tablature since it would make things look messier than they needed to be. Play it in 16th notes.

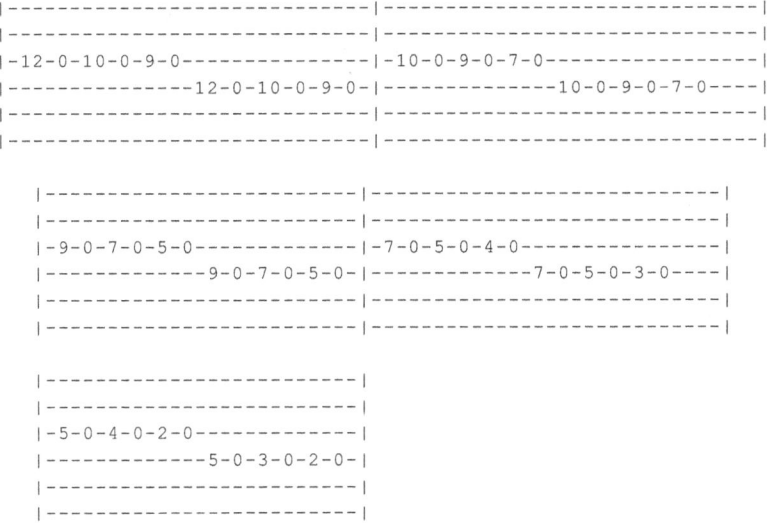

This is probably the nicest sounding lick out of the three open strings licks I have described. It possesses a classical feel due to the pedal point, and the transitions between the D and G strings adds an exceptional and captivating attribute.

Tremolo Bars & the Wah-Wham Technique

I have never been especially fond of using tremolo bars although I did experiment quite a bit with one for a couple of years. I learned to do the various bombs and dives with artificial and pinched harmonics and I could use one to add nice subtle vibrato to notes and chords. But I never trusted a whammy bar in live situations. My guitar always seemed to go out of tune.

How to Become a Guitar Player from Hell

Probably because I never had one of the really expensive types of tremolo systems.

 Edward Van Halen is an expert with a tremolo bar and Joe Satriani is a master with one as well but Steve Vai I think is the best user of a tremolo bar. He invented many new tricks and techniques. He would also use them in extreme ways, such as pulling the bar around behind the bridge and yanking on it and shaking quite hard as if he were trying to break the entire apparatus off the bridge. Satriana was also innovative with tremolo bars, I recall the technique he invented called "lizard down the throat" in which he would hit a note on say, his G string around the 2nd fret, then slide his finger toward the higher frets while gradually depressing the tremolo bar as in a dive, and it would produce a thoroughly "sick" and disturbing sound, which I guess to him sounded similar to someone sticking a lizard in their mouth and swallowing it – "lizard down the throat." Try it out. Move your sliding finger slowly while depressing the bar gradually. Experimentation will be required to get the correct sound. You may enjoy the lizard down the throat technique enough to use it during a solo on one of your next country and western cover songs. If you do, be careful because it may cause a few seizures, random flash knockouts, and paroxysms of anarchy to occur in the audience. Be sure to crank up your amp's distortion all the way before cramming any lizards down people's throats.

 There is another technique that can be used with a tremolo bar that I invented, which is quite experimental in nature. It is called the Wah-Wham technique and I believe I created it since I have never seen anyone else use it. I only employed this method during rehearsals with one particular band and never had the nerve to try it live. It is an avant-garde practice that produces an almost insane sound of swirling chaos. Sonny Sharrock would have probably loved it (Sharrock was a "free jazz" guitarist know for his noisy, unorthodox and loose playing style). The way the Wah-Wham method works is you use both your tremolo bar and wah-wah pedal simultaneously to produce off-the-wall sounds of depravity, beauty, and dementia. Because phrases and licks produced by the enigmatic Wah-Wham method can not truly be transcribed, I will have to explain it in algorithmic form.

 1. Begin by playing a few common licks or phrases, anything at all, perhaps an improvisation using the common Blues or minor pentatonic scale.

 2. Now press down on your wah pedal to turn it on and begin rocking it back and forth in a slow steady motion, it doesn't matter how you manipulate it, but move the pedal around in some manner.

 3. Next, while picking notes and playing the licks of your solo, hold the end of your tremolo bar in your hand and push down on the bar at random intervals in your improvisation, raising it up and pressing it down, shaking it

and manipulating it as you continue to pick notes in whatever way that strikes you, even in random or haphazard ways.

4. Continue playing licks and rocking the wah-wah pedal back and forth and raising and depressing the tremolo bar; add in more sophisticated licks and keep moving the wah pedal and tremolo bar simultaneously in different ways at the same time.

5. Listen to the ensuing chaos and beauty and depravity coming out of your amplifier.

6. Become astonished and enlightened and let the grievous otherwordly sounds inspire you to take control of your life and behavior and to contemplate your existential relation to the universe and how you can improve it and help other people in need.

The Wah-Wham method outlined above is definitely a bizarre technique. Perhaps too wild or "out there" for a guitar player to actually use on an album or even to play live. I experimented with this method during a handful of rehearsals with one particularly "open minded" band whose members were tolerant of extreme music, and the drummer seemed especially impressed by it, during breaks in one rehearsal he followed me around asking me how I was making those depraved sounds. The Wah-Wham technique. It is special and ripe for more experimentation and investigation and I invented it. I had never seen a whammy bar and wah pedal used in conjuction before. But then I quickly let the technique go because I didn't use tremolo bars live so I thought no one would ever hear it. The Wah-Wham method was used only a few times during one summer before I quit that particular band and I have never used it since. My main guitar today is still not equipped with a tremolo bar so I don't plan to experiment or develop the technique further.

So readers, I give the Wah-Wham method to you. Feel free to use it however you like. Play around with it, modify it, add it to your guitar repertoire and your musical knowledge. Let your inhibitions fall away and create some quality music with it to release all your heartfelt emotions lying deep within you.

Exotic Scales for Flair and Panache

Exotic scales from other countries or cultures are wonderful and can add a great deal of flair and spice to your playing. I used to love stumbling upon a new exotic scale to learn. And I still do. But they are somewhat difficult for laymen to find in the traditional musical literature and rarely pop up in books or magazines.

I remember when I was around 15 going to the library to pour over music history and theory books searching for the strangest and most exotic scales I

How to Become a Guitar Player from Hell

could find to impress my friends and enemies, but at that early stage I did not know how to read music well enough to transcribe the scales I found, then work them out on the guitar in a way that made sense. So I waited and collected a couple of exotic scales as the tablature appeared in various sources and years later I returned to the library and managed to procure a few more and now I have included four of the best exotic scales below that I think sound incredible when used in improvisations. There are of course many more exotic scales out there but I want to leave some of the joy of discovery to you.

For three of the scales below I have included background rhythm examples that you can play behind the scales if you think they are worthy enough. Knowing the exotic scales isn't everything, you have to know how to use them in your music to get the most out of them, which means your band members are probably going to have to provide some type of accompaniment and you will need to instruct them on what to play. The background chords were built by simply taking various notes from the listed scales and laying them out on the fretboard. Another way to establish an overall tonality for playing the scales over is to simply have another instrument drone the root note as you play the scale and then establish the major harmonies through the notes of your improvisation. I have found that a "thin" background accompaniment actually sounds better to me when using exotic scales.

I also changed up the keys for each scale given below (well, two are in the key of A) since I wanted the reader to be able to hear the different flavors they possess, which is somewhat difficult to do if they are all listed in, say, the key of G and played one after the other.

Our first scale will be the Gypsy guitar scale, or the Hungarian Gypsy minor scale as it is also known, in the key of A. This one has a dark and elegant sound. It was a favorite of the famous gypsy jazz guitar player, Django Reinhardt, who possessed incredible natural talent and ferocious technique despite having the use of only the first two fingers of his fretting hand after being badly injured in a fire when he was 18 years old. Django regularly incorporated the Gypsy guitar scale into his jazz improvisations, combining it with other scales and arpeggios in superbly musical ways.

```
Gypsy Minor in A

|----------------------------4-5-7----|
|----------------------4-5-6----------|
|----------------4-5------------------|
|-----------6-7-----------------------|
|-------6-7-8-------------------------|
|-5-7-8-------------------------------|
```

How to Become a Guitar Player from Hell

Even though the intervals in the scale are quite unusual (notice the three semitones in a row for example), the scale is surprisingly easy to play, falling naturally under the fingers.

Here is a sample background rhythm you may want to have a guitarist perform as accompaniment. All its notes come from the Gypsy Minor scale. For this rhythm part I am basically holding the same chord shape and arpeggiating the notes in a certain pattern. The chord, if played normally, would be an unusual A5add#9add♭13 chord. That is, an A fifth add sharp 9th add flat 13th chord.

```
|-----------------|--------------------|
|-----------------|----------6---------|
|-----5-------5---|-----5---5---5------|
|---7---7---7---7-|---7---7-------7----|
|-0-------0-------|-0------------------|
|-----------------|--------------------|


|-----------------|-----------0------|
|-----------------|----------6---6---|
|-----5-------5---|-----5---5--------|
|---7---7---7---7-|---7---7----------|
|-0-------0-------|-0----------------|
|-----------------|------------------|
```

You could have another guitarist (or even another instrument such as a keyboard) repeat the four bars above as you play over it using the Gypsy Minor scale. The arpeggiated chord could be palm muted or allowed to ring. When you improvise with the Gypsy scale, be sure to milk those three consecutive semitones and put as much feeling into them as possible while imagining yourself travelling through the countryside in a Gypsy caravan filled with gifted musicians playing sublime soul-churning music.

Our next exotic scale is the Arabian guitar scale in the key of A. It has a nice finger pattern easily memorized on the fretboard. Some harrowing, freakish, and staggering melodies can be produced with this one.

```
Arabian Scale in A

|-----------------------------4-5-7----|
|---------------------------4-6-7------|
|-------------------4-5-7--------------|
|-------------4-6-7--------------------|
|-------5-6-8--------------------------|
|-5-7-8--------------------------------|
```

And below is an example of two chords constructed from its scale tones, although I admit I don't think these two chords sound especially great or represent traditional Arabian music in any way, I am only listing them here as examples of how chords can be built from tones of the scale you are working with. Feel free to invent a better sounding rhythm part than the following, it shouldn't be too difficult.

```
|---------------|---------------|
|-----7------7--|-----6-----6---|
|-----7------7--|-----5-----5---|
|-----7------7--|-----4-----4---|
|-5-5----5-5----|-0-0---0-0-----|
|-5-5----5-5----|---------------|

|---------------|----------------|
|-----7------7--|-----6------6---|
|-----7------7--|-----5------5---|
|-----7------7--|-----4------4---|
|-5-5----5-5----|-0-0----0-0-----|
|-5-5----5-5----|----------------|
```

The first chord could be classified as an A 6th Suspended 4th chord while the second could be considered an A Minor 6th Sharp 5th.

Our next scale is the Japanese scale in the key of G (yes, I finally switched keys as I promised earlier) and I have not included any backing chords for this one, so the reader can consider it an exercise to generate their own accompaniment to match the scale (plus, I am not exactly familiar with any type of Japanese music so I am sure I would only be butchering a proper background tonality if I offered chords of my own).

```
Japanese Scale in G

|---------------------3----|
|-----------------3-4------|
|-------------2-5----------|
|-----------5--------------|
|-----3-5-6----------------|
|-3-5----------------------|
```

This one is rather difficult for me to play and memorize since its fingering is so unusual, but it does contain the most exotic intervals so far and I like how the scale sounds. Usually during solos I will transition into this one after playing a few phrases in the Phrygian mode, just to shock people. Just to scorch their ear drums a little. Just to provide the audience with a bit of razzmatazz. Yes, you can go into any of these scales while soloing over the chord changes of your normal songs, they will provide a stimulating jolt and sound like you are playing "outside," which you will be most of the time, and the audience will surely pay a lot of attention to you as you're provoking their ear drums.

How to Become a Guitar Player from Hell

Our last exotic scale will be the Jewish guitar scale. Strangely enough, it is also known as the Spanish Gypsy scale. This one is really a doozy and one of my personal favorites.

```
Jewish Scale in D

|-----------------------------------------10-11----|
|-------------------------------10-11-13-----------|
|-------------------------11-12--------------------|
|------------------10-12-13------------------------|
|--------9-10-12-13--------------------------------|
|-10-11--------------------------------------------|
```

I have listed it in the key of D to demonstrate a technique very effective for playing droning type background chords while improvising with exotic scales over the top. What you do is detune your low E string a full step so that you are in "Drop-D" tuning. Then our backing rhythm for the Jewish scale will consist of a low droning D note and two scalar phrases incorporated near the end of each bar to generate a slightly hypnotic effect. Here is the tablature for the background riff:

```
(In Drop-D tuning, the low E tuned down one whole step):
                         ~                                ~
|--------------------------|----------------------------|
|--------------------------|----------------------------|
|--------------------------|----------------------------|
|--------------------------|----------------------------|
|---------9-10-12-10-9-10--|---------10-12-13-12-10-12--|
|-0---0--------------------|-0---0----------------------|
```

The rhythm of this is in common 4/4 time and the riff performed by hitting the detuned E string twice in quarter notes for sustain, then adding in little phrases from the Jewish scale toward the end of each bar in whatever phrasing you choose. Your rhythm guitarist or bass player can change the ending licks around, of course. The detuned E to D has a nice effect since you can play notes of the Jewish scale while allowing the low D note to ring and hence hear how the different tones sound in relation to the droning background pitch. Remember that when playing in Drop-D tuning you will have to move the notes of the scale that occur on the low E up two frets so they will be in tune. That is, the notes on the 10th and 11th frets on the low E in the original scale will now be played on the 12th and 13th frets.

Improvise using the exotic scales above and enjoy the ineffable and compelling melodies you produce. Let the unusual intervals of the scales work their magic on audiences lucky enough to hear music from different cultures.

How to Become a Guitar Player from Hell

Muted Harmonics

Admittedly, this is a technique that I never used even once during a live performance. Muted harmonics are a somewhat advanced technique and I never felt confident enough to pull them off during a gig. I believe they were invented by Edward Van Halen but I'm not sure. To execute muted harmonics consistently is fairly difficult and you will need an excessive amount of gain on your amp as well as delicate hand placement for the notes to sound out correctly. But when done right, muted harmonics sound as brilliant as sparks flying off a grinding wheel as it shaves metal off a carburetor in a master mechanic's garage.

Start off with this three note lick, playing it continuously, similar to a trill (a trill is two notes played in rapid succession, while below we have three).

```
|---------------------------|
|---------------------------|
|--4p2p0h4p2p0h4p2p0h4p2p0---|
|---------------------------|
|---------------------------|
|---------------------------|
```

Now comes the difficult part. As you trill the notes, mute the strings near the bridge lightly with the very edge of your palm, and then move it toward the nut of your guitar. You will have to mute DELICATELY so the harmonics will pop out clearly. Do not mute the stings nearly as much as when you play crunchy guitar riffs. When you are moving your palm and it arrives between the pickups, this is the best location for the harmonics to burst out with clarity and volume. When muting you want to find the best hand position and pressure so the dampened harmonics explode from the strings with force and lucidity.

That is the basic technique behind playing muted harmonics.

But the concept can be greatly expanded upon.

Incorporating more than one string is one way to modify it. Using the middle finger of your picking hand to mute the strings near the bridge is another.

Try this variation I invented:

```
|-------------------------------------------|
|-------------------------------------------|
|-h4p2p0h4p2p0------------h4p2p0h4p2p0----------|
|--------------h4p2p0h4p2p0------------h4p2p0h--|
|-------------------------------------------|
|-------------------------------------------|
```

How to Become a Guitar Player from Hell

Now instead of using the edge of your palm for muting, we will use our middle fingers instead. I find when using my middle finger I can mute with more subtlety, but it can still be tricky. Don't be afraid though. Fight through the fear and lightly place your middle finger (hand palm-down) across the strings near the front edge of your bridge pickup and mute it by lightly touching the strings there as you continuously trill the notes. Start moving your middle finger toward the neck pickup. Once your finger arrives over that pickup, slowly begin moving it back toward the rear pickup again and keep trilling with your ring and index fingers the entire time. Again, you will need a lot of gain on your amplifier and a lot of experimenting with the muting to get the harmonics to sound out well. Also, because now you are trilling across two strings, you will get a wider range of harmonics, but simultaneously the muting will become more difficult and you will have to be even more subtle about finger placement and movement. Much practice with this technique will be necessary before you can play it accurately and consistently during a live performance. (Also, extraneous string noise will of course be a problem with this technique. Make sure to dampen the other strings properly to keep them from ringing out as you trill and slide your middle finger around.)

Muted harmonics are a fantastic effect, but quite puzzling to most people upon hearing them (when I first witnessed Eddie Van Halen playing them during a solo on his *Live Without A Net* video, I had no idea how he was producing that magnificent, bright, trebly shower of notes. Only later did I see someone else executing muted harmonics and it dawned on me that Eddie was doing the same thing). To reiterate, I never once used this technique during a live performance. I did not think I would be able to pull them off cleanly and with enough volume. In fact, I still don't think I'd be able to play them even now. But perhaps you can.

Finger Exercises

I have read that many guitar players do not like performing finger exercises, just as some people do not like eating big bunches of bright green vegetables. They say finger exercises are boring or see them as a chore to be endured which may only slightly enhance their finger strength and overall dexterity after too much work.

But I am an anomaly in this regard.

I love finger exercises.

The thought of improving my accuracy and increasing the speed and timing in my hands and brain and the enhanced dexterity and bulging finger muscles that comes from only an hour or two of playing finger exercises with a metronome gives me a wonderful feeling of accomplishment and productivity.

How to Become a Guitar Player from Hell

There can be a few drawbacks with finger exercises, however, since they come in many forms: some musical; most not. You should practice the musical variety as much as possible, although the nonmusical kind are also of value. But I'm of the opinion that one shouldn't play nonmusical finger exercises too often because I believe they have the potential for damaging one's ears, even if only slightly. That is, if you play them too much and thus hear chromatic notes for hours everyday, it may affect your ability to generate good musical sounding melodies later on. Of course I cannot prove this, it is just my gut feeling.

Nevertheless, to thoroughly contradict myself, we'll start off with a nonmusical sounding finger exercise first. Play this one using all four fingers of your fretting hand and pick every note. Once you have completed one ascent or one descent of the pattern, slide the finger you end with forward one fret to the next position and continue the pattern.

You should be able to see how the pattern repeats itself on up the neck: once you hit the fourth fret on the high E string, slide your pinky up to the fifth fret and start the descent. After you work your way up to the twelfth fret in this manner, you should descend using the same pattern. I recommend starting off using eighth notes at about 120 beats per minute, then work your way up in tempo.

I began with this nonmusical finger exercise to illustrate a point. That you should use it only moderately. Don't perform it every day. Why? Listen to how it sounds. Not good. Use some of the following musical finger exercises instead if you want to increase your speed and agility by playing exercises more often. For years I practiced the above finger exercise at the beginning of every practice session and now I wish I wouldn't have. At that time, in the early stages of learning the guitar, the chromatic sound of the lick didn't bother me at all. Which is not a good sign. It should have sounded ugly to me. Now I think I would have been better off playing proper scales at the start of

How to Become a Guitar Player from Hell

each session, which I believe would have improved my musicality and ear for music considerably. But it is too late now. However, I can warn you though: I believe you should play melodic finger exercises as much as possible in the early stages of learning guitar so your sense of "musicality" is not affected. I don't actually know if chromatic based exercises are harmful to any degree, but I know I don't like the sound of them now; yet (to reiterate) at the beginning stages of playing, I thought they were fine. So use any nonmusical finger exercises in moderation and focus instead on exercises that belong to legitimate scales or arpeggios.

Now we will move onto a rather simple classical sounding finger exercise that does possess some semblance of musicality. Start by playing it as eight notes and work up to sixteenth notes. This exercise is in the key of A minor.

```
|-10-13-12-13-10-13-12-13-8-12-10-12-8-12-10-12-|
|-----------------------------------------------|
|-----------------------------------------------|
|-----------------------------------------------|
|-----------------------------------------------|
|-----------------------------------------------|
```

```
|-7-10-8-10-7-10-8-10-5-8-7-8-5-8-7-8--|
|--------------------------------------|
|--------------------------------------|
|--------------------------------------|
|                                      |
|--------------------------------------|
```

Once you finish playing the two measures above, shift back to the 10th position and continue repeating the lick until your fingers become stiff and tired, then take a short break. Keep going until you feel you can't possibly continue, but still push on for a few more repetitions! Being careful not to strain the muscles in your hand, of course.

A variation on the above exercise is one in which we keep the classical sounding pattern, yet instead of descending on a single string, we shift to a lower string, like so:

```
|-10-13-12-13-10-13-12-13-----------------------|
|-------------------------10-13-12-13-10-13-12-13-|
|-----------------------------------------------|
|-----------------------------------------------|
|-----------------------------------------------|
|-----------------------------------------------|
```

How to Become a Guitar Player from Hell

```
|------------------------------------------------|
|------------------------------------------------|
|-9-12-10-12-9-12-10-12--------------------------|
|----------------------9-12-10-12-9-12-10-12-----|
|------------------------------------------------|
|------------------------------------------------|

|------------------------------------------------|
|------------------------------------------------|
|------------------------------------------------|
|------------------------------------------------|
|-8-12-10-12-8-12-10-12--------------------------|
|----------------------8-12-10-12-8-12-10-12-8---|
```

Now to finish off this chapter we will journey back into the dreaded nonmusical territory and play a chromatic sounding pattern up the neck. With this exercise you should use a rolling motion with your fingers, applying and releasing tension evenly so every note on each string will be articulated cleanly and you don't get any extraneous guitar noise. Note that this finger exercise also doubles as a sweep-picking lesson!

```
|--------6-3-------------7-4-------------8-5-------------9-6--|
|-----5-----4---------6-----5---------7-----6---------8-------|
|---4---------5-----5---------6-----6---------7-----7---------|
|-3-------------6-4-------------7-5-------------8-6-----------|
|-------------------------------------------------------------|
|-------------------------------------------------------------|
```

Continue up the fretboard in the same fashion.

Remember to work with a metronome when performing these licks. Start off slowly but gradually increase the tempo while still maintaining a comfortable playing level, yet strive to push yourself beyond your capabilities near the end of each session. Before stopping for the day, return to an easier tempo and play through the exercises again once or twice for a "cooling down" period.

I recommend playing these and other finger exercises at least once a week (I would usually perform them every other day, myself) and soon your fingers will be soaring so fast over the fretboard your bandmates or musical colleagues will be utterly in awe and think you're either a robot, an extraterrestrial, or totally superhuman.

Extreme Lick #2 - Double Stops and Tapping

One of the things I like to do for the Extreme Licks chapters is take two different guitar techniques that seem to have nothing in common and combine

How to Become a Guitar Player from Hell

them to make one weird lick. That is the basic idea behind this extreme lick – using double stops and finger tapping together. When considered individually, these techniques seem very different to me. Yet by using them together we can create the effect known as SYNERGISM. Sometimes combining two disparate parts of anything, musical ideas, writing ideas, painting ideas, compositional ideas, even physical objects such as chemicals or food ingredients, can occasionally produce an effect greater than the original sum of its parts. This is known as synergism. A powerful force filled with agape love, moving tenderness, and supreme splendor. Now let's create some synergism right this second.

We will begin with double stops in the key of D minor. (The D minor pentatonic scale will be used throughout most of this extreme lick, with some Dorian mixed in.) Next we will switch to fast tapping with wide stretches, and you want to strive for a real contrast between the double stop beginning, making each part sound totally different, then we will return to the double stops with a "walk" up the pentatonic scale chromatically. I like this extreme lick very much even though it is longer than the others. Switching between double stops and tapping produces a striking, singular effect.

```
          ~                      ~
|--------------------|--------------------|
|-12p10-12p10----10--|-12p10-12p10----10-|
|-12p10-12p10-12-10--|-12p10-12p10-12-10-|
|-------------12-----|-------------12----|
|--------------------|--------------------|
|--------------------|--------------------|
                                   ~
|-13-12-10-------------------------|
|-13-12-10-13-12-10----------------|
|---------13-12-10-12p10-12b14r10----|
|------------------12p10-12b14r10----|
|----------------------------------|
|----------------------------------|

   T           T           T
|-17p15p13p10h17p15p13p10-------------|
|------------------------17p15p13p10-|
|------------------------------------|
|------------------------------------|
|------------------------------------|
|------------------------------------|

   T           T           T
|-17p15p13p10h17p15p13p10-------------|
|------------------------17p15p13p10-|
|------------------------------------|
|------------------------------------|
|------------------------------------|
|------------------------------------|
```

How to Become a Guitar Player from Hell

```
              T          ~                                    ~
|------------|----------------------------------10--|
|-17p13b15---|-------------------10b12r10--------|
|------------|----------10-11-12-10b12r10-12-----|
|------------|-10-11-12-10-11-12----------12-----|
|------------|-10-11-12--------------------------|
|------------|-----------------------------------|
```

Performance tips: because you will be switching back and forth from picking double stops to finger tapping with very little time in between transitions, you will probably have to execute the taps with the middle finger of your fretting hand while continuing to hold the pick between your index finger and thumb. That is how I play this extreme lick for ease of position changes. Also, the middle tapped portion can be extended longer than what is transcribed. I usually play it for quite a few bars.

Keep in mind also that the phrasing in the tablature above is not entirely accurate. It is just a bare outline for you to go by. In reality, I would improvise much more with the double stops also, interchanging them with a few single note pentatonic licks and bending more notes with vibrato before going into the tapping part. I would also alter the phrasing of the tapped licks as well, using more rhythmic patterns in the passage. As already mentioned, this is one of the drawbacks of using strictly tablature in a book, certain rhythms and proper phrasing cannot be adequately expressed most of the time. Nevertheless, I hope you get the general idea.

Mastering the Smaller Frets

Depending upon the size of your fingers, smaller frets on the neck may be rather difficult to "finger" or fret with precision. If you have a guitar equipped with 24 frets and your fingers are large and thick, playing notes in the upper range may take some getting used to. My main guitar is a B.C. Rich Warlock model with 24 frets and the higher range is rather difficult for me to play on cleanly and consistently if I don't practice in that portion of the neck regularly.

One way to master the smaller frets is to simply focus on them a lot in your practice sessions and frequently play scales there. By not neglecting the upper register, you will be able to slide up and wail away at any time with supreme confidence. Don't neglect the upper register, give it the proper attention it deserves.

Below is the B Major scale an octave above its normal location at the 7th position. Play through it many times, up and back, performing many variations on the notes in between while attempting to be as precise as possible with your finger placement and the execution of each pitch.

How to Become a Guitar Player from Hell

```
|-----------------------------------------------21-23-24--|
|---------------------------------------21-23-24----------|
|--------------------------------20-21-23-----------------|
|------------------20-21-23-------------------------------|
|----------19-21-23---------------------------------------|
|-19-21-23------------------------------------------------|
```

 The fingering I use for the B major scale in this position is exactly the same as if I were playing it in the 7th position. The lowest notes on the E and A strings are played with my first, third, and pinky fingers, while for the notes on the D and G strings I use my index, middle and pinky fingers, then for the B and high E strings I use my index, middle and ring fingers, respectively. If you find the B Major scale too difficult to play in this higher position, move it back a whole step or two to get A major or G major and practice with those scales instead.

 Another way to practice using the higher frets is whenever you are playing one of your favorite licks or phrases in its normal location, probably somewhere in the middle of the neck, think about transposing it to the higher frets in the extreme upper portion, say around the 20th fret or higher, and see if you can play the lick equally as well there. Simply move your normal licks into the upper register and practice them there and soon you will learn to master those pesky upper frets and get your big bony fingers conditioned to being cramped up into such a tiny space.

 Also, here is one final lick that is somewhat bizarre or outrageous, (but remember that is one of my goals in this book, to give you information you would not normally encounter in any other guitar book). If you want to get a little flamboyant or scandalous, you can use your front pickup as another fret! Attempt a few licks in this extreme higher position and if your front pickup is set up correctly, you will see that fretting on it is possible and can be quite musical. I have the front humbucker on my Warlock set up so that whenever I want to use it as a higher fret I can easily do so, (I believe playing on it is equivalent to having a 30th or 32nd fret, somewhere around there).

 My front pickup is tilted so that it is aimed down in the front (the portion closest to the fretboard) and raised higher in the back. The angle is drastic enough so that when the strings are pressed down they "fret" out cleanly to produce normal yet extremely high-pitched notes. You can probably set up your front pickup in a similar manner so that your strings hit at the back edge and create a type of "pseudo-fret." (I suppose you could also tilt your pickup the other way so that you have a pseudo fret at say the 27th or 28th position, but I have never tried it.)

 Here is a lick made up of easy descending triplets that incorporates the idea of using your front pickup as a higher fret:

How to Become a Guitar Player from Hell

```
             ~           P           P           P           P              ~
|-21-23-21--21-23-30-23-21-30-23-21-30-23-21-30-23-21-23--|
|---------------------------------------------------------|
|---------------------------------------------------------|
|---------------------------------------------------------|
|---------------------------------------------------------|
|---------------------------------------------------------|
```

    Note that I have used 30s with a 'P' above them to stand for "pickup," marking when our pseudo-fretted notes are to be played on the front pickup. Just press the string down past the fretboard and if you have your humbucker set up correctly it should produce the desired note.

    The lick above is simple and more flashy than substantive although it does have genuine musicality. If you play it live a few audience members may really get a kick out of seeing your supple fingers stretch past the fretboard to grab notes on your humbucker to produce pitches so high they make their wisdom teeth ache. The lick is a legitimate musical phrase even though the idea behind it may seem flamboyant or scandalous. I like the technique quite a bit and usually use it at least once during a live performance to really freak out the chicks at the front of the stage.

"Outside" Playing

    When soloing or improvising, guitar players normally stay within certain scales that fit the chords or key of the song they are performing, or at least they try to play phrases that match the overall tonality of the tune. But because there are no "rules" in music, only what sounds good or bad to one particular individual, which is of course entirely subjective, occasionally players will go "outside" the normal scalar patterns and play various notes to achieve more nontraditional or angular and dissonant types of melodies. Mostly this is used in jazz music where sophisticated chords go by at supersonic speed and the player is trying to keep up with them, and when they play outside of the normal key it doesn't sound nearly as harsh as when they do so over just one tonality, as in a rock song, for example.

    Adding jazz influences to rock music is a cool thing (which was done to perfection by guitarist John McLaughlin and perfectly exemplified in his band *The Mahavishnu Orchestra*), and one simple way to add an outside flavor to your music (even though this book is not intended for jazz players, we can still use some of their techniques) is to merely shift up one fret from the scale you would normally be playing in and use the same pattern to execute a few notes in the "wrong" location, then you can quickly return to your normal scale. Playing out of key for brief moments can sound unusual or exotic or wicked, depending upon your taste, and it will also provide a real jolt to listeners. But

How to Become a Guitar Player from Hell

remember that you will want to return to your proper scale immediately afterward unless you really want to wreak havoc on people's ear drums, which is also fine in some cases, especially if you are playing for an audience that loves country music (only joking). Going back and forth, in and out of scale may sound pretty easy, but to do it effectively and smoothly and also instantly whenever the thought happens to enter your mind can be challenging indeed. If done accurately and with passion, the outside melodies you generate can make you sound like a cool jazz bebop cat who can improvise better than Charlie Parker after he just hocked his friend's furniture for a double dose of heroin.

Our first example of playing outside will involve the C major scale. We will simply play a few notes, shift down for the first outside phrase, then head back into C major territory, follow it up with a quick chromatic descent, then end with partial scale fragments to achieve a wide interval sound.

Here it is.

```
                              ~
   |-13-10-12---------------------|
   |----------13-12-10-8----------|
   |---------------------10-9-----|
   |-------------------------10-9-|
   |------------------------------|
   |------------------------------|

   [--outside--]           [---outside---]
   |=============================|------------------------------|
   |-----------------------------|------------------------------|
   |--------8h9h11-12-9----------|------------------------------|
   |-8h9h11-------------10-9-----|------------------------------|
   |-----------------------------|-11-10-9----------------8h10-|
   |-----------------------------|--------11-10-9-12-8h10------|

                       ~
   |----------------12h13----|
   |-----------12h13---------|
   |------9h10---------------|
   |-9h10--------------------|
   |-------------------------|
   |-------------------------|
```

Notice that I go out of key at the beginning of the second measure (marked above) but I'm continuing to play the normal pattern for C major there, except I have lowered the fingering a half step so I am on the wrong frets, and then I also go out of key at the beginning of the third measure by playing a simple chromatic run. The rest of the lick is straightforward C major. The last hammered doubles are just partials of the C major scale to create a wide interval sound, which I like. I don't believe the transcription above is a great improvisation or particularly special in any way, it is just there to give you an

How to Become a Guitar Player from Hell

idea of how to go in and out of scales you are working in to give your playing an "outside" flavor.

Of course you can use any scale for shifting up or down a half tone to creating outside sounds, but the key to doing it well is to get the in-and-out transitions as smooth as silk (Jimmy Herring is a master of this). Pentatonics may be the easiest scales to start with.

Our next example is an outside lick in E minor. Say you are wailing away over an E7#9 groove, you can start off with a few bluesy bends and vibrato in the 15th position, then perform a shimmering chromatic "glissando" lick to get you back to the original 12th position E blues box so you can blast away with some more grievous bends. When doing the pull-offs, try to make them really pop out of your guitar so they sound like glass shattering.

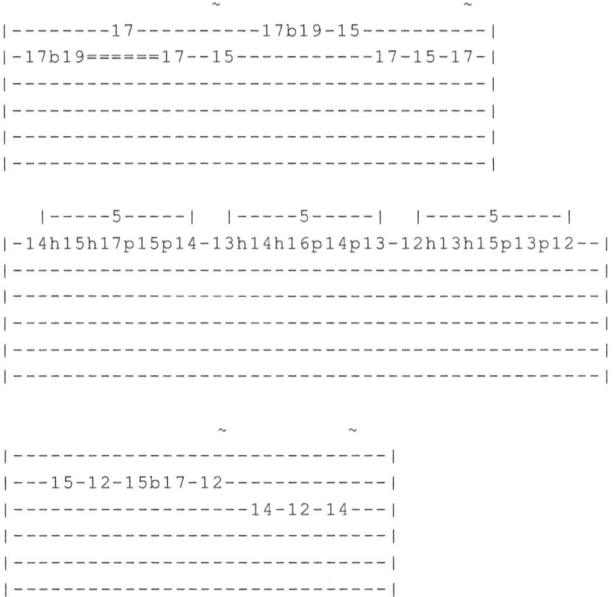

The descending quintuplets at the start of measure two make up the glissando lick and the instance of outside playing in this phrase (you could start them at the 15th position and play 15-16-18-16-15 on the high E at the beginning, then continue with what is transcribed to have 4 quintuplets and a longer glissando), notice they have 5's above them as they are to be played as quintuplets, but with that said they should also be performed "crammingly," which again means very quickly without worrying about the exact phrasing of the notes. The lick is simply an index, middle, pinky finger (1-2-4) combination that is moved downward for three frets, and the chromatic nature of the lick will sound 'outside' and similar to a shimmering cascade, but since

How to Become a Guitar Player from Hell

it goes by so quickly it will not do too much damage to the ears but only wake up a few headbangers who may be dazed or daydreaming in the audience. Since it sounds so jazzy you can pretend you are John Coltrane bombarding the audience with a wall of atonal sound in a small New York jazz club as you're playing it.

Another way to play outside is not to shift up or down at all, but simply use a different fingering from the scale you are working in at that moment, then switch back. For example, say you are playing in B minor pentatonic, you can switch to a different pattern right in the middle of the scale, then return to the pentatonic, like this:

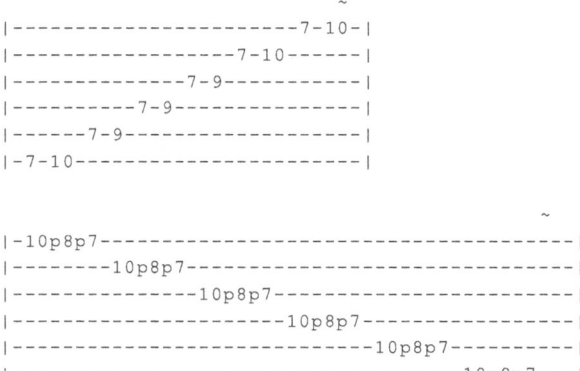

With the pattern above, not all of the notes will be outside, but enough of them will be to produce a jazzy outside effect.

While the above lick is relatively easy to play, remember your goal with these patterns and licks is to make outside playing sound as MUSICAL as possible. With some practice it will be easy enough to simply run chromatic patterns all over the neck and then switch back to the proper key, but that isn't your main priority. You need genuine "music" to be coming out of your amplifier at all times, so you will have to add phrasing and subtle nuances and personality to express whatever feelings are swirling around inside your body and mind. Try to get the licks and patterns to sound fluid and natural so you can create compelling music with them instead of merely generating a bunch of annoying chromatic noise. Practice the simple transitions above extensively so when you are in the middle of a solo you can just think of going outside and immediately execute seemless jazzy runs to delicately twist a few ear drums, then return to the proper key and resolve the sticky situation satisfactorily.

How to Become a Guitar Player from Hell

Alteration of the Blues and Minor Pentatonic Scales

I have discussed the blues scale previously, it is an important scale in music, and there are many ways musicians have altered it over the years to suit their specific tastes and needs. In this minichapter I will give you two other versions of the blues scale, both of which are based on the minor pentatonic scale.

Also, before I list the scales, I should say that if blues is not a style of music you are currently listening to, or one you don't listen to at least periodically, it should definitely be on your to-do list. Blues is a popular and expressive form of music perfect for improvisation. There are some truly astounding guitar players in the blues realm, such as Buddy Guy, Albert King, R. L. Burnside, Mississippi Fred McDowell, Stevie Ray Vaughan, Junior Kimbrough, Robert Johnson, Lightnin' Hopkins, T-Model Ford, and others. Check them out and absorb their rhythms and soul and passion and learn everything you can from them. You won't regret it.

Our first alteration of the blues scale will be to simply add one extra note to it:

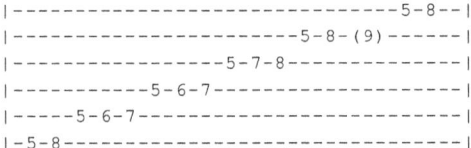

Notice the note was added at the 6th fret on the D string, which is a grace note between the root and seventh (a half step lower than the root). This variation comes in handy when doing walks up the scale but you can also land on the added note and milk it for a second to get a different type of blues sound. Try it out and see if the scale works for you. (Notice the G# note in parentheses, which is an octave above the added note; of course it is part of the scale but I never play it there.)

Our next modification involves the minor pentatonic instead of the blues scale. It is based on a simple discovery of my own – (that is, I had never seen the scale expressly written out in the following manner before I started using it, although I am quite sure I wasn't the first to discover this particular modification). When playing blues progressions in E, I would occasionally land on the major third (even though I was using the minor pentatonic) and I would notice how bluesy it sounded. So I adapted the minor pentatonic to include the major third as a passing tone. Here it is in the key of E:

```
|----------------------------------------12-15----|
|------------------------------------12-15--------|
|----------------------12-13-14-------------------|
|----------------12-14----------------------------|
|------(11)-12-14---------------------------------|
|-12-15-------------------------------------------|
```

As with our first modified scale, the G# note on the 11th fret of the A string is surrounded by parentheses because I usually don't play that note even though it is part of the altered scale. I play the G# on the 13th fret G string most of the time instead.

I actually like the second altered scale better, the one with the major third, since it sounds bluesier to me, although your taste of course may be different. Try to invent your own variations of the blues and pentatonic scales based on what sounds good to you.

Finger Picking

As I have previously stated in this book, I have never been particularly fond of learning sophisticated rhythm guitar techniques or practicing rhythm playing extensively, because I was always more interested in soloing and becoming a good lead guitarist. This attitude also extended itself to the technique of fingerpicking. Although I am fairly proficient at fingerpicking now – I practice it regularly and can play a decent version of "Stairway to Heaven" as well as other less famous songs – it was never my strong suit or a technique I looked forward to sitting around practicing for many hours.

But again, this is the wrong attitude to have and you should try to learn from my mistakes. Rhythm playing and fingerpicking are both very important aspects of learning to play the guitar. To be honest, I should have practiced fingerpicking every day in the early learning stages, but in those days I was primarily interested in becoming a **Rock Guitar God** rather than a tame folk music guitarist.

Folk music is mainly where fingerpicking was developed and used and I was never a big fan of folk music, although now I have great respect and admiration for anyone who can fingerpick well. There are a few excellent fingerstyle guitarists out there who can make their guitars sound like entire orchestras and it is truly impressive.

Even though I am not the greatest fingerstyle player in the world, I am going to give you some gentle tips on the proper way to fingerpick. First, we will start off with a simple lesson. With fingerpicking you primarily use your thumb and the first three fingers of your fretting hand to pluck the strings. To get the proper feel for the technique, let's first fret a normal A minor chord and begin arpeggiating the notes (picking them individually) in the following pattern.

```
A minor

|---0-------0-----|---0-------0-----|
|-----1-------1---|-----1-------1---|
|-------2-------2-|-------2-------2-|
|-----------------|-----------------|
|-0-------0-------|-0-------0-------|
|-----------------|-----------------|
```

Use your thumb to sound the low A note, your ring finger to pluck the high E note, the middle finger to sound the C note on the B string, and your index finger to pluck the A note on the G string. It is an easy pattern and here you are mainly trying to get the feel of using your fingers to pluck. Speed it up slightly with your metronome if you like.

Next, let's use another chord, E Minor this time, and continue the same arpeggiated pattern using the same fingers to pluck with, except now we will have to move our thumbs down one string to sound the low E, and then we'll alternate between A minor and E minor. Notice the strings played for the E minor chord are just open notes and you don't have to fret anything at all!

```
E minor and A minor alternating

|---0-------0------|--0--------0-------|
|-----0-------0----|----1--------1-----|
|-------0-------0--|------2--------2---|
|------------------|-------------------|
|------------------|-0-------0---------|
|-0-------0--------|-------------------|
```

One of the main things to keep in mind when fingerpicking is that you are trying to develop as much control as possible over the fingers of your picking hand. You will want each finger to be as independent and strong as possible and to be "conscious" of its own position and location on the strings at all times. Also, when positioning your picking hand over the strings, you should hold your hand almost perpendicular to the strings. You don't want your hand tilted at any sort of angle, since your fingers may accidentally hit or brush against adjacent strings that way. Other than that, you simply have to practice fingerpicking a lot until it becomes natural to you. Control and precision and confidence with plucking the strings is what you are shooting for here. Finger picking can also test your coordination considerably since in many instances you are moving the fingers of each hand simultaneously.

So there you have some very basic information on how to get started fingerpicking.

One more thing. Another method of practice I should have taken up during the early days of learning to play guitar would have been to simply gather up all my picks, transport them to a friend's house, then return and play my guitar all day without the assistance of any plectrums. Anything I would have wanted to play I would have been forced to use only my fingers on the strings. I believe that would have helped me learn fingerstyle quickly and efficiently and if for some reason I ever dropped a pick during a live performance I would have been confident in my plucking ability for a short time until I would have been able to procure another pick.

There are many famous guitarists who have employed fingerstyle exclusively and perhaps if you get acquainted with their work it will inspire you to take up finger picking in a way I did not. Wes Montgomery and Duanne Allman are two excellent fingerstyle guitarists who come to mind, while Tuck Andress is another more recent player who can execute sophisticated chords and compelling melodies simultaneously to make his guitar sound almost identical to a full symphony orchestra.

So even though I am far from an expert when it comes to fingerpicking, there you have some basic tips and advice to get you started. I hope you find it of value and that you practice finger picking frequently and assiduously.

Extreme Licks #3 - Finger Stretching Patterns

As we learned only a few chapters ago, some incredible "outside" sounding licks can be generated by using uncommon fretting patterns and simply shifting them up or down adjacent strings while retaining the same basic shape. This outside effect is doubly enhanced if you stretch your fingers to grab notes that don't usually belong to any traditional scalar patterns. Eddie Van Halen frequently used this idea, and later Dimebag Darrell did as well (Darrell was the guitar player in Pantera tragically shot and killed onstage by a fan).

Let's start off with a lick inspired by the playing of Dimebag Darrell (although he never played the following lick exactly as written below, as far as I know).

```
   PM------------------------------------------------|
   |-3--| |-3--| |-3--| |-3--|   |-3--| |-3--| |-3--| |-3--|
   |--------------------------------|--------------------------------|
   |--------------------------------|--------------------------------|
   |--------------------------------|-----------------8-9-12-8-9-12-|
   |--------------------------------|-8-9-12-8-9-12-----------------|
   |---------------8-9-12-8-9-12---|--------------------------------|
   |-8-9-12-8-9-12-----------------|--------------------------------|
```

How to Become a Guitar Player from Hell

```
        PM------------------|  ~
   |-3--|  |-3--|  |-3--|  |-3--|
   |---------------8-9-12-8-9-12---|
   |-8-9-12-8-9-12-----------------|
   |-------------------------------|
   |-------------------------------|
   |-------------------------------|
   |-------------------------------|
```

Execute this lick as quickly as possible in a series of palm muted triplets that move up in pitch. Use your first, second, and pinky fingers to reach the notes. Moving your thumb far under the fretboard will help you grab the notes on the 12th fret if your fingers are not particularly long or limber. Another nice lick similar to the one above is to start on the high E note at the 12th fret and play descending triplets in the same pattern while working your way down to the low E string. (The descending version is actually easier for me to play for some unknown reason.)

Our second finger stretching pattern is more extreme in its outside sounding flavor and incorporates an even wider stretch. Here are the basic notes we will be using:

```
|-18-15-12------------------------------------|
|----------18-15-12---------------------------|
|-------------------18-15-12------------------|
|----------------------------18-15-12---------|
|-------------------------------------18-15-12----------|
|----------------------------------------------18-15-12-|
```

Although I won't provide any actual "licks" for this "scale," I will list below a sample "composition" to show how it can be used. You should think of the original pattern as a sort of "diminished" scale for use in your improvisations when you want to get a little barbaric or unhinged. The thing to focus on here is retaining the same pattern from string to string. (Note: Usually I will not play any of the 18-15-12 notes on the A or E strings, as those stretches are a little too extreme for my hands.) But this one really has a unique outside sounding quality to it, worthy of exploration. Of course you can shift the pattern around to get different "keys" also.

Here is my sample "composition" which is just a suggestion for a way the pattern might be used (you don't have to follow this note for note):

```
|-12-15-18-15-12----------------------------------|
|----------------18-15-12-15-18-15-12-------------|
|--------------------------------------18-15-12-18---|
|-------------------------------------------------|
|-------------------------------------------------|
|-------------------------------------------------|
```

```
|-12-15-12----------18-15-12---------------------|
|----------18-15-12----------18-15-12----------15---|
|----------------------------------18-15-12------|
|-------------------------------------------------|
|-------------------------------------------------|
|-------------------------------------------------|


|----------------12-15-18-15-12----------------12---|
|-18-15-12-15-18----------------18-15-12-15-18------|
|-------------------------------------------------|
|-------------------------------------------------|
|-------------------------------------------------|
|-------------------------------------------------|


|-15-18-15-12-------------------------------------|
|------------18-15-12-----------------------------|
|--------------------18-15-12-18-15-12------------|
|----------------------------------------18-15-12-|
|-------------------------------------------------|
|-------------------------------------------------|


|-------------------------------|
|-------------------------------|
|-------------------------------|
|-------------------------------|
|-18-15-12-15-18-15-12-------------|
|--------------------18-15-12-5--|
```

Notice the wide interval sounds that seem to make sense musically even though the piece is based on an "outside" finger pattern, and also that it sounds quite classical when played with conviction and puissance.

3
Miscellaneous Advice

A Good Way to Practice - (Method Two)

Having already detailed one practice method in this book (one that involves partitioning the day into sections devoted to various guitar techniques), here is yet another method I would frequently use for many months at a time, hardly ever splitting up my day into various time slots devoted to single topics. But before I explain the actual method, first we need a little background information.

During the course of my guitar playing "career" I encountered a few wayward individuals who were not familiar with the best way(s) to practice. Instead, they would announce they were going to embark on a practice session and go into another room and play a few riffs, then run through a couple of old licks that had been part of their repertoire for years, jam their way through a couple of tired and weary chord progressions, then put their guitar in its rack and head out the door to the bar.

You will not progress much as a guitar player if you do this.

One highly effective and entertaining way that I have found to practice is to learn songs you like with the aid of tablature from a magazine or the internet (there is a lot of free tab on the net, although most of it isn't as accurate as magazine versions done by professionals with good sound equipment which is used to slow down difficult guitar parts). Here is what I recommend:

1. Go to a store with a few guitar magazines and leaf through them until you chance upon a song that seems interesting enough to learn (one with a good guitar solo is better than one without, of course) – many quality guitar magazines have good transcriptions of new and classic songs.

2. Hopefully you already have the CD with your song on it so you won't have to go out and buy one.

3. Put your CD player in a room with your guitar, amp, and a music stand; place the guitar tablature in front of you on the music stand.

4. Listen to the song at least two times completely through without touching your guitar. (When learning songs, I would make the mistake of playing parts of the song without having listened to the complete tune thoroughly first, which caused me in some cases to end up playing a different version of the song and skipping many necessary details and subtleties in the original).

5. Open your magazine and look at the tablature that concerns the main chord sections or riffs of the song. Play through them a few times holding the sound of the original song in your head, until you think you can play the riffs well enough to jam along with it on your CD player.

6. Once you have the main verse and chorus sections down, concentrate on the solo (you did pick one with a solo, didn't you?). Listen to the solo twice all the way through without picking up your guitar. Now slowly work your way through the tablature trying to play certain sections of the solo without the CD

playing. When you feel you have quite a few of the main parts down, try to play along with the solo. If you don't hit every single note, it is all right, you can perfect it later. For now just focus on getting through the main parts, and then you can break down the difficult parts you need to work on and study how to play them. (Most professional musician's solos will be beyond your abilities during your first few years of learning guitar.) Remember to refer back to the tablature as much as you need to for the especially difficult sections and try not to get discouraged with techniques beyond your present level. On the other hand, after a lot of practice and many trips through the entire solo, if you feel you have it down perfectly, then practice trying to execute it even better than the lead guitarist in the band! Or you can throw in extra techniques of your own to make the solo even more advanced.

    7. Once you feel you have all parts of the song down well, play it through from beginning to end, attempting to really nail every note without making any mistakes.

    With enough practice, gradually you will be able to play along with the song you have chosen just as if you are another guitar player in the band.

    That's all there is to this second type of practicing. Do you know what you are doing if you practice rock and metal songs that appeal to you in this manner? Do you know what it ultimately means if you are learning a Guns-N-Roses song off of *Appetite for Destruction* or a song from *Master of Puppets* by Metallica? It means you are practicing with some of the greatest bands in the history of music! What could be better for improving your playing? AC/DC, U2, The Rolling Stones, Megadeth, Led Zeppelin, Rush, Rage Against the Machine, Mahavishnu Orchestra, Slayer, Fugazi, Pink Floyd, Jimi Hendrix, Black Flag, Shakti, these are excellent bands to be in the company of! Learn from them. Absorb their grooves. Soak up their phrasing and dynamics and the sick notes of their wicked solos. Get down and trip out with the big dogs cuz it's party time heavy metal and punk rock style. I can't tell you how many times I put on *Appetite for Destruction* and played through every single song, over and over again without stopping, sometimes jamming through the whole album five times. I knew every rhythm part and every fill and every solo. I also played along with Satriani and Metallica albums in the same way, (although I think I skipped a few songs here and there on those albums). Learning songs off of your favorite CDs is one of the most enjoyable ways to practice the guitar and in my opinion you will be picking up almost the same level of real life band experience by jamming along with these top-notch musicians.

    But of course I don't think you should use this method of practice exclusively. Devoting time to singular topics whereby you focus more on specific techniques is also greatly beneficial and in fact necessary for becoming a true guitar player from hell.

How to Become a Guitar Player from Hell

Equipment

When it comes to equipment I have always been of the minimalist school. For many years I would play gigs in bars using only a Crate half-stack amplifier and a cheapo off-brand electric guitar with moderately high action that a friend traded me for lifetime bass lessons. I used no effects pedals, no tremolo bar, no guitar tuner, and the only distortion I had was what came with the amp. (For a clean sound I would turn the volume down on my guitar.) That was it. (Although later I did start using a wah pedal.) I loved this simple setup and I kicked much ass on stage and I moved many people to tears with my rhythm grooves and improvisational solos.

Overall I wanted my sound to come from my hands and mind and my heart and soul.

I still do.

Most effects pedals I tried back in the day always seemed to sound artificial and generic, so I avoided them. Also I never was one of those technically minded guys more interested in ordering new equipment and scouring pawn shops for good deals on gadgets than actually playing my instrument. All I wanted to do back then was practice a lot and play as many live gigs as possible and learn how to play the guitar using the best and most advanced techniques so I could fulfill all my musical potential.

But if you are a technically minded person who enjoys looking for new additions to your sound with various pedals and electronics and whatnot, if you love collecting new equipment and adding it to your setup, by all means continue searching and exploring since you never know what might help you express yourself better. Try out every piece of gear you are interested in and buy every gadget your paycheck will allow. Try to find whatever works for you to get as close as possible to that perfect guitar sound in your head.

The coolest effects pedal I ever heard was on a record (I forget the title) with Tommy Bolin on guitar and whenever he would play a solo he would hold a note and manipulate the knobs or buttons on some type of effects box and the note would acquire a vibrant swooshing sound similar to a rocket blasting off into outer space and then there would be a few explosions in the background. I am not sure what the pedal was called or exactly how it was used but that was the only effects pedal other than a wah-wah that ever sounded interesting to me.

How to Become a Guitar Player from Hell

Improvisation

Imagine. You're on stage. Your favorite guitar is slung over your shoulder. The crowd is over a thousand strong. Spotlights are shining down. Sweat is falling from your face, streaming down your arms. You are in the middle of one of the best solos you have ever played in your life. Your heart is pounding and your foot is tapping to the beat and you feel euphoric and energized and high and every musical idea that enters your mind, every sound and nuance necessary for full self-expression, your fingers and hands instantly execute to absolute perfection. Nothing feels better than this.

Suddenly you feel like going into some fluid legato patterns and you play them in 64th notes and then transition into some gut-bucket blues phrases in the middle of the neck and then you move further down and throw in a few slow low bends on the E string that really provoke the audience, you can see two women in the front row flinch, then you squeal out a few pinched harmonics on your D string and start sweep-picking through minor seventh arpeggios in the upper register. Next, you cleanly transition into some finger-tapping licks and by then you feel totally lost in the music. You are swaying back and forth and your eyes are rolled back and you begin headbanging as your nimble fingers soar over the fretboard and your feet pound the stage. You are almost mesmerized by the sounds coming from your guitar, you feel free and unhinged and your body sways and your fingers fly with abandon, finesse, and excitement.

Improvisation in music is the spontaneous creation of melodies and phrases (some players are even adept with chords) usually while in performance. The musician responds immediately to the background accompaniment, his environment, his inner feelings and overall emotional state to immediately invent new music. Improvisation when done well can transport the audience and the musician to other planes of consciousness and existence. It is one of the most wonderful and exciting things about playing the guitar and being a musician. Improvisation can also border on being a mystical and religious experience with self-discovery and true fulfillment thrown in, but it can also be extremely frustrating if you run out of fresh ideas and your playing gets stale. A good improvisation, however, will always remain one of the most fascinating and moving things about playing music. The challenge of creating something unique and beautiful on the spot is a noble pursuit every serious musician has great respect for.

Over time, as you learn more about playing the guitar, you will gradually acquire more and more licks and melodic patterns and phrases until before you know it you will have a full collection of musical ideas at your disposal, ready

How to Become a Guitar Player from Hell

in an instant to put together to make up a solo. You will have a full repertoire of ideas you can call upon during the spur of the moment while improvising.

At first, in the initial stages of learning to improvise, you can simply string together a collection of finger patterns, short licks, melodies and exercises that you enjoy, as long as they are in the correct key, and more than likely you will make up a few interesting and entertaining solos with them. But later you will want to move past this stage. In your improvisational endeavors you should attempt to transcend the method of simply inserting different licks and stock phrases you have memorized into a certain key so they fit the song you're playing.

The main goal with true improvisation is not to rely on any preconceived melodic patterns or licks worked out in advance. The real objective is to create something extraordinary that you have never played before. This is not easy. Of course modifying and expanding phrases you already know is one form of improvisation, but if you really want to spontaneously create something no one has ever played before you will have to move beyond preconceived licks.

You will have to stop yourself from playing rote licks when they pop up, which will take much practice and energy, but it is possible. You may be able to achieve true improvisation at some point, once you have reached a certain level of technique on the instrument and have studied enough theory and scales, then you may be able to create your own musical phrases on the spot.

A long time ago I read a magazine article on Alan Holdsworth in which he said that after he reached a certain level of ability on the instrument, and noticed that he was repeating a lot of the same phrases, he consciously stopped improvising in the manner of compiling licks and would not allow his fingers to fall into any patterns he had played before. He would force his fingers to move differently every time they touched the fretboard. He had to practice this new method a lot but eventually arrived at a level to where he could create entirely new phrases almost every time he improvised. However, Allan Holdsworth is a rare musician and one of the best jazz fusion players on Earth. He is a truly monster on the guitar, almost superhuman, but you can still heed his example and attempt (for a few minutes of each practice session anyway) to never allow your fingers to fall into familiar patterns while improvising.

John McLaughlin is another incredible improvisational player. He once formed a band called Shakti with classical Indian musicians solely to perform their live improvisational excursions that succeeded in transcending space, time, and causality. Some of their performances were so great reviewers said that when watching the band perform it seemed that the musicians were actually levitating above the stage with their instruments, penetrating and destroying the normal barriers of banal reality.

That is the goal.

That is the ideal to aim for.

How to Become a Guitar Player from Hell

Improvisation can not really be taught, you simply have to learn it as you go by jumping into the deep cruel bottomless vortex of reality and start flailing to swim or at least float your way out. You have to blitzkrieg and pursue and annihilate and just **GO FOR IT**. But remember that improvisation is one of the most regal acts a human being can undertake so you must have flawless intent.

Improvisation can occur in groups as well. One of my fondest memories of playing guitar is walking into a room with an excellent drummer and a great bass player and without saying a single word to each another we would start playing and follow each other's leads and execute different riffs and melodies and grooves by merely picking up on what the other players were doing. To begin the session, one of us would start jamming a riff or phrase and the others would fall in and we would play and listen to each other and change riffs and add dynamics and splashes of tone and color and back each other up and hit cymbal crashes and change to fast and slow sections and take solos at some point and it felt extraordinary, surreal, and inspiring, and I loved every second of the experience. Freedom. True musical freedom was achieved on a few occasions.

During one of these improvisational experiences, I remember a trumpet player coming to our jam session. He began playing with us, improvising, and it was fantastic and one of the best events I can recall about my musical career. You see, I always wanted to have a jazz fusion type of band so I could trade solos and play funky scratch rhythms and long harmonized melodies with a horn player. The trumpet player who came to our jam session was a friend of the bassist's. They knew each other from college. They took many musical classes together. We were already playing in the drummer's house and the trumpet player simply rode up on his minibike and took his trumpet out of a little black bag strapped to his seat, came in and started blowing away and I was very impressed. I listened to him closely and when I started improvising my own solo I could feel that the normal way I would phrase melodies had changed. Then I got the idea of trading solos with the trumpet player. I tried to get his attention but he didn't notice me in the background, he was too busy swaying and playing his butt off with his eyes closed. Nevertheless, the music we created that day was special and spectacular. I wish one of us would have had the sense to record it.

So in summary, if I had to provide you with a few tips on learning how to improvise, even though I believe it cannot really be taught, I would say for the first two or three years you should concentrate on learning as many licks and stock phrases as possible. Then gradually start stringing them together into the same key and use them in your solos. After a couple of years of this type of improvisation you should make a conscious effort to stop playing common phrases and licks that you have played previously. Gradually your improvisations will be a mix of stock phrases and true improvisation, that is, musical ideas no one has ever performed before, then at some point you may reach a state where you can play true improvisations anytime you want. But it is a rare thing attainable by only the best and most dedicated musicians.

On Bands

After you have been playing electric guitar for a few years (or even for a few months, as in my case), you will probably want to get into a band or form one of your own. The most difficult thing about forming a band is finding dedicated members. You probably won't find greatly talented players right away (it is difficult to find people truly talented at anything), but you can still have fun as long as the people you choose for band mates are willing to come to practice when they say they will. When individuals are not getting paid to keep their bodies in a certain physical location for a specific amount of time, they tend to not stay there for very long, or even show up in the first place, since they have trouble envisioning some type of payoff in the future. But don't get discouraged, because usually you will be able to find a few decent people trustworthy enough to start a band.

I have been in about ten or twelve bands during the course of my existence on this planet (some of their names are listed in my Bio at the end of this book) and I found all my members or joined bands that already existed simply by word of mouth. Some musicians go into music stores and put advertisements up on bulletin boards or they answer ads they find in magazines, musical newspapers, or zines, but I never tried that method. It may be effective, I don't really know. I do know however that the best players in any community will be known by their having established a reputation as a good or great player on their particular instrument. Everyone talks about the hottest musicians in their communities and eventually word gets around. Although now, with recent technology entering the picture, such as the Internet and Myspace, I bet it is even easier for good players to find each other and be willing to rehearse and play gigs and be serious about creating a good successful band. You would think so, anyway.

Once you do get into a band, as with any relationship, there will usually be problems that arise. Some of which could be problems with alcohol, theft, homemade drugs, promiscuous girlfriends, egotistical megalomaniacs, flakeouts, sexually transmitted diseases, delusions of grandeur, rip-off artists, illiteracy, extreme halitosis, selfish assholes, acid flashbacks, bongs, rampant dishonesty, practicing only one day every two weeks for one hour, bad skin conditions, rabid dogs biting into your calves, dirty rehearsal spaces, people claiming to be band managers when they're really only short order cooks at the local greasy-spoon diner, getting into the groove of summer – all these can

How to Become a Guitar Player from Hell

be terrible problems that will cause your band major setbacks on your way to getting inducted into the Rock-n-Roll Hall of Fame. Also "Band Funds" can be a lot of trouble, I recommend avoiding those at all costs.

Here is some advice about how to be a good band member:

Buy your own equipment. Practice as much as you can. Be willing to make sacrifices for your band. Treat everyone with respect. Do what you say you are going to do. Learn as many cover songs as possible. Write original material. Be dedicated and driven. Try to be creative at all times and remember the importance of improvisation and also having fun. Help your band get gigs. Walk around and put up fliers. Don't complain a lot or be negative in any way. Spread the word about how fantastic your band is. Develop a good sense of humor. Save up your money. Buy a van. Go on tour. When you have a gig, play as hard as you can. Pretend you are going to literally die if you don't put on a good show for your audience, try to shatter your body into millions of pieces with the ferocity of your songs and solos.

Let's say you have tried to form a band and you are having trouble. Not enough people are showing interest in your ad, or you can't find enough decent players in your area, or no one can afford to purchase a drum set. Do not despair because you may be able to start a band with only two people. Yourself and one other person. I always wanted to experiment with a two-man band. Here is the way I would have done it.

1. Buy a drum machine for the rhythm parts of your songs.
2. Get another person adept at playing keyboards or some other instrument – it should be a melodic instrument to add to the music and thicken the sound, a trumpet or horn would work.
3. Start a two-man band.

A band with only two members would be interesting and highly advantageous for many reasons. Due to the limitation of members and instruments, it would probably force you to come up with an entirely new sound. Also it will be less people necessary for showing up for rehearsals and also more money from gigs for each person. One member would probably have to sing to add to the entertainment value, but the drum machine would supply all the backing rhythm, and with yourself on guitar the riffs and solos would be covered, and hopefully the other person could play some type of instrument to add to the sound. Plus there would be plenty of space for improvisation. With this type of minimal band you probably wouldn't sound like the hundreds of other same-sounding bands out there. I got the idea for this after learning about *Suicide*, a great innovative two-man band with only a singer, and an instrumentalist playing a keyboard and a drum machine. It is something to think about if you are having trouble finding band members.

Phrasing

Beautiful melodies. Those are what I aim for now in my playing and improvisations. But that wasn't always the case. In the early stages of learning guitar, I focused almost exclusively on speedy and technical over-the-top playing. I thought lightning fast licks and scary technique were the only things worth aiming for. But now, playing the right notes, perhaps only a few, over the perfect set of chord changes, which hopefully causes the listener (and player) to feel a plethora of strong emotions is the most important goal for me. Enticing and inventive melodies are what I strive for, although I do use speed on occasion since it can be a great way to express a certain amount of passion, or other feelings such as anger, excitement, yearning, bliss, frustration, terror, jealousy, whatever. Now I realize speed should be used moderately and tastefully.

So here are three main points that concern phrasing to close this ultra-short chapter, as well as some advice from Miles Davis:

A. Speed is occasionally necessary, but I feel it shouldn't be the most important thing in your playing.

B. Hitting the "right" notes over a good set of chord changes is a noble goal to have.

C. Ultimately each guitar player is different and if you feel that focusing exclusively on extreme techniques and speed should be the most important thing in your playing, by all means follow that instinct and see where it takes you.

Finally, to very loosely paraphrase Miles Davis on the subject – (I wish I could quote it exactly and give you the proper source, but my searches have turned up nothing) – this is something I memorized long ago, which is probably greatly altered from the original by now: "When soloing, don't play too much. Let your music breathe. If you have something to say, say it right then, don't blow a feeling. Leave your phrases unfinished and hanging. Leave something for the imagination."

Taking Care of Your Hands

Making sure that you do not damage your hands or fingers is of course extremely important if your goal is to become a professional guitar player. But in my opinion you do not have to go to any great lengths to keep from using your hands, such as refraining from opening doors or jars, not turning keys in locks, not typing letters or turning pages of books, not shaking hands with shovels, not pushing away middle-aged women with your fingertips when they try to kiss you at gigs, as I have read some players do. Using your hands and fingers for a few activities such as typing or using keyboards may actually increase your playing ability by building up certain muscles in your fingers.

Just make sure you do not do anything extremely dangerous, such as getting your hands too close to heavy machinery with many moving parts and revolving gears. And don't get upset with your girlfriend and slam your fists into walls and break your knuckles (as I have done), because the walls and doors will always be victorious in the end. You will also have to keep your fingernails rather short on your fretting hand, and the index finger and thumb of your picking hand (also your middle finger if you tap with it). Other than that, you should be fine.

Remember that if your fingers are all bent-up, gnarled, bruised, twisted and damaged, you will have trouble playing those sublime melodies and divine chord progressions you want to share with the world. Although Django Reinhardt's fretting hand was badly burned when he was 18 years old (as I've mentioned in another chapter) and afterward he was forced to use only the index and middle fingers of his fretting hand, he still went on to become one of the best jazz guitar players the world has ever known, but chances are you do not possess the musical genius he did and hence you will not fair as well in your guitar playing career, so you should take proper care of your hands. But who knows, maybe you are a musical genius on your way to attaining immortality with the guitar. I hope you are and that this book helps you greatly along the way.

String Care

When I first began playing guitar, I didn't know anything about the various string gauges. Hence I ended up practicing for many hours a day on a cheapo Silvertone electric that was purchased at a pawn shop and equipped with heavy .012 gauge strings that pulled the guitar neck forward and put many a large white blister on my finger tips. Not pleasant at all.

Gradually I learned that these heavy gauge strings were not necessary and even detrimental to the life span of my guitar, not to mention my ten precious digits. So I bought some light .009 gauge strings at a music store and couldn't believe the difference in playability. Lighter strings are much better for the beginner. (I assume most readers are already familiar with different string gauges so I won't explain how they are measured.) Over the years however, I tried out different kinds of strings and came to prefer the heavier .010 gauge. I liked the extra "fight" in the action and the slightly heavier feel and the richer tone.

How to Become a Guitar Player from Hell

Whatever gauge you happen to choose, taking care of your strings is important. After each practice or playing session it is recommended you wipe off the moisture and dirt using a clean cloth or towel (make sure not to use your step-daddy's filthy grease rag). Wiping the strings down after playing will greatly increase the life span of your strings and also help them retain that initial "bright" sound for awhile longer. Although after a few weeks, if none of your strings have broken by that point, and depending upon how much you have practiced with them, they will most likely be "dead" and need to be changed.

When first putting strings on your guitar, as previously mentioned you will notice their bright and metallic sound. Many guitar players like this tone, but I do not. In the first few hours after changing the strings, the tone is too bright and trebly for my taste. Only after they have been stretched and played for two days or so do they reach the point of having the perfect tone for me.

Also, after many practice sessions and several weeks have passed, you may notice that your B and E strings are "warbling" in pitch. This is a strange effect. Whenever I used to get warbling high strings in the early days of playing, I would still try to execute every note of a solo as cleanly as possible to eliminate the warble. Of course it was impossible and my thinking slightly absurd (which was pointed out by a singer in my band after he asked why I didn't just change my warbling strings), but I guess that is just the type of person I am; yet I also think it may have actually improved my accuracy a bit. However, if you are going to have a gig the next day and your strings are warbling, you should definitely change them.

Organizing Band Rehearsals

You should organize your rehearsals before they take place. Bands should always plan out what they are going to work on beforehand. You will improve your productivity a hundredfold if you list what to work on before each rehearsal starts – your band will accomplish tons more in the long run. Make a list of all the things you want to do prior to the rehearsal and write them down on paper. Designate one band member to make the list before the next rehearsal starts and always take turns making the list. At the end of each practice session, state who will make the schedule the next time. Or if one member doesn't mind doing it all the time, they can be the official rehearsal organizer. Here is one example of a typical practice list.

1. Warm up with two easy cover songs, say, "Sunshine of Your Love" by Cream, "Walk This Way" by Aerosmith, or play more recent songs, as long as they are simple to play.

How to Become a Guitar Player from Hell

2. Work for one hour or more on a new cover song that the band is trying to add to their set list (write the actual title of the song down on paper), e.g. it could be: "Master of Puppets" by Metallica. (Hopefully the individual band members listened to the song or practiced it beforehand, which would mean you have "dedicated" band members, a very rare type – hold on to them.)

3. Miscellaneous work. Jam on new riffs, help the vocalist add melodies to an original song, work with the bass player on nailing a difficult odd-timed groove with the drummer, write some original music, help each other with musical problems, write fantastic melodies, become musical geniuses, work to procure million dollar record deals. It could be anything, but plan it out on paper first.

4. Play two or three of the band's favorite songs, ones that are easy to perform, as a cooling-down "fun" period; or just jam on favorite songs or riffs while the singer practices his dance moves. Whatever you want, as long as you are playing together for awhile and it isn't too strenuous.

5. You are finished. Go home.

That is a sample list for a fairly productive three to five hour band rehearsal, depending on what you do during the miscellaneous section. (Also remember to take short breaks between segments for water and snacks.)

Making a list of what you need to work on before each rehearsal starts definitely beats everyone standing around saying, "Hmm, what do you guys want to play next? I wonder what we should do now? What do you think we need to work on today? Hey, when are we supposed to be ready for that upcoming gig in front of that Taco Stand? How come God didn't tell us what we should be working on today during our drive over to the rehearsal space? Where did you buy those new shoes, Johnny? What time is it anyway? All right, where is that hamburger with barbecue sauce I left on this counter? Your dog isn't going to run downstairs and clamp on to my leg again, is he? What did you call me?"

Precious hours can drift away while these absurd and useless questions are bouncing around the room.

Don't let it happen to you and your band.

Hopefully, if you do organize your rehearsals in this manner, your other band members will retain some of what you worked on during this time. Of course occasionally no matter how much you rehearse, no matter how much you think your band members are learning the material, it still won't do you any good, for example, once I formed a band with some friends, and we got a gig set up at another friends' house, we started rehearsing in the drummer's garage, the band was a trio, the drummer doubled as the singer, I was on guitar of course, and the bass player also sang back-up vocals, we rehearsed for four days a week, 1 PM to about 6 PM (two of us were unemployed, the other worked the night shift), five hours a day four days a week for about 6 weeks

How to Become a Guitar Player from Hell

we practiced, getting ready for the big gig, a party where at least a hundred people were expected to show up, the friend said we would get free beer, and maybe a little cash as payment (which meant we wouldn't get paid anything).

The day of the gig arrives. We're ready. Been practicing our asses off for weeks. We have 30 cover songs. Pop and metal and classic rock. Also ten original songs. We are proud of them. There's only about twenty people at the party. We start playing anyway. The drummer chokes on the first song. Forgets most of the lyrics. Then he fouls up the second song. Turns the beat around twice. He stumbles through the third song. He's really nervous. Choking under the pressure, to use a cliche. He keeps making mistakes. Can't stop. Messing us up. I get pissed off. Think about stopping and walking out and going home. But after awhile I start to calm down. Focus on just playing my best. We take a break. During the second set the drummer starts to relax. He plays a little better now. Still not very many people at the gig. I don't care. I stopped taking it seriously a long time ago. I start giggling at the drummer's mistakes. Who gives a shit.

Then I notice that something is going on with the bass player he guzzled a lot of alcohol between sets. He isn't playing the correct bass lines anymore he is also taking big shots of whiskey and drinking beer and people are passing a mysterious pipe around and he is taking long swallows from another bottle and I have no idea what's in it. The bass player is getting plastered I start watching him he isn't playing any of the bass lines I taught him. Instead he starts soloing on his bass throughout the riffs of our songs, I stare at him he is really out of it. While the drummer is playing and we are supposed to be backing him up the bass player's fingers have moved up very high onto the upper frets of his bass he is dancing around the room not following the beat or me and he is soloing atonally throughout all of our songs that we worked so hard on. Dancing around soloing dancing and jamming out prancing and soloing on his bass guitar he is totally drunk. All those weeks spent cramming bass lines into his head, all that time helping him get the songs down, it is now gone. The last two sets are a complete debacle the numerous rehearsals the abundance of hours that I could have been doing worthwhile activities such as improving my own playing all of it is down the drain. Oh well what can you do.

I got depressed. The gig was a total failure. Not many people showed up anyway. We didn't get paid a dime. Later the drummer got drunk and high and started imitating body slams and pile drivers from the fake championship wrestling matches they put on tv that I hate. I prefer mixed martial arts. The drummer eventually dives onto the floor and bends his wrist backward, almost breaking it. We don't practice for months after that. He couldn't play his drums. Would have been useless anyway. The band breaks up. A real tragedy.

How to Become a Guitar Player from Hell

So the moral of this story is not only do you have to try to find dedicated band members, you also have to find ones you can trust to perform well when the pressure is on during live gigs. You don't want your band members cracking or wigging out when it's time to perform, and you don't want them getting drunk and soloing over the riffs to your songs (especially if you are getting paid to play). It isn't easy to find good band members. But it is possible sometimes.

Did you notice that I broke many punctuation rules in the anecdote above? I like doing that. But I also did it to make a point. You don't always have to follow rules. Any rules. Writing rules, music rules, painting rules, math rules, sculpture rules, any kind of rules. Even a bumblebee breaks the rules of physics when it flies. So apply this idea to your guitar playing. In solos you can play notes that are outside the scale or overall tonality (see the Outside Playing chapter), or you can use irregular phrasing or do whatever the heck you want. There is no right or wrong. There aren't any definitive rules in music. Either you convey some type of emotion and produce something that somebody wants to listen to you (maybe only yourself), or you do not. Just as a person can write in many different styles, you can also play solos and riffs in numerous ways. It is fun to experiment and try different things. Remember this basic idea and use it in your solos, riffs, and anything else you play or do.

Listening

There is an art to listening. Close listening. Studious listening. Vigilant listening. You have to listen well and frequently if you are going to be a musician, any kind of musician. Once I asked a drummer what type of music he listened to and he said, "I don't listen to other people's music, I make my own, and I listen to only that."

No. Do not be like this. It isn't right. It won't help you. Listen to other artist's music and listen closely to the nuances and vicissitudes it contains and absorb the sounds as intensely as your ear drums will allow. Try to develop perfect pitch so you can play whatever you hear in your head that sounds good. To be honest, I do not have perfect pitch, but it would have made my life much easier as a guitar player if I would have been blessed with it. In another chapter of this book I will give you brief lessons on how to improve your ear. But that is a different kind of chapter than this one. Here I am telling you that you should listen to music carefully and frequently and concentrate whenever you do so, I am not describing how to improve your ear, but simply saying to listen well to what other musicians are doing and pay attention to how they are doing it and dissect their sonic alchemy and ask what happens when they play and if you could reproduce the sounds they are making.

How to Become a Guitar Player from Hell

You may want to pretend that listening to other music isn't important and try to turn yourself into a guitar player from hell in other ways such as using various larger-than-life or brutalist characteristics. You may want to pretend you are some kind of badass macho innovator with no concern for the musicality of others, but it won't work because you still must know how to listen carefully to become a true guitar player from hell.

One mistake I used to make in my early days of learning to play the guitar was that I would get too impatient when learning a new song and start trying to play a song BEFORE I had even LISTENED CAREFULLY to every detail of the song (which I have already written about in the A Good Way to Practice – Method Two chapter). Hence, I would end up making subtle changes to the riffs and solo parts and they would not be true representations of the music I was trying to learn. Of course it is okay to slightly change music and songs to fit your own style if you have one and if you think you have something better to add to the music, (or even if you do not have anything better to add, it is still okay) but in the early learning stages you really should try to improve your technique by learning to play other people's music as well as you can.

Again, when learning new songs, I recommend putting your guitar in another room and sitting down and listening closely to the song you want to learn at least twice all the way through before even picking up your guitar, so that you do not change the riffs frivously in certain places, even if it's only slightly. Do not get impatient. There will be plenty of time to play and practice the song later on. Initially you should concentrate on absorbing the details and nuances of the music before you start riffing away or shredding through the solo licks.

As far as improving your ear it will become better over time as you pay close attention to the chords and notes of various songs (see also my chapter on Improving Your Ear). Ideally, you should reach a level to where you can figure out the basic key of any song along with say about 80% of the chords used. The act of transcribing different songs you like is also beneficial. You shouldn't always rely on tablature.

Also, in everything you listen to, no matter what type of music it may be, rock, country, metal, reggae, opera, rap, swing, calypso, jazz, country, hip-hop, classical, bluegrass, yodeling, ska, punk, skiffle, grindcore, whatever, try to find something good in the music, at least one salient quality of beauty or pathos and think of how you might incorporate that same element into your own playing and songwriting. Be open-minded. Soak up the sublime and beneficial aspects of other people's music and let their sonic expression float freely through your mind and maybe someday the nice parts will come out in your own writing and improvisations, but only after they have been filtered through your heart and soul and individually stamped by your authentic and inimitable personality.

How to Become a Guitar Player from Hell

Developing A Style

Ernest Hemingway created his own prose style. So did Gertrude Stein after being inspired by Picasso and his painting method known as Cubism. Lamborghini developed his own style of making cars. Aleister Crowley developed his own way of doing **MAGICK**. And Nike has their own style, sort of. They each achieved their styles while working in different mediums, but now whenever someone mentions their names people familiar with their work get a mental picture of what each of their brand's style entails. This is an important goal to strive for, but I'm afraid there is no way it can be taught. Some guitarists develop their own styles naturally, as Kieth Richards did by simply practicing on a tour bus as he traveled from concert to concert listening to records by famous blues legends that he worshiped and plunking around on his acoustic or telecaster, while other guitarists learned extensive theory and practiced finger exercises and exotic scales and chords in college class rooms for numerous hours every day, as Steve Vai did, while other guitarists took private lessons and learned from records as I believe Yngwie Malmsteen did. Yet they each achieved radically different styles on the instrument and when people familiar with their music hear them they immediately know which is which and who is who.

You should try to create your own guitar style, too. Or maybe you should not consciously try to do it, but just let it flow naturally and narcotically out of your system. Get in touch with your individuality, pay attention to the elements and styles of music you're instinctively drawn to, celebrate them and elaborate on their influence and inducements and let their characteristics come out of your fingers on your guitar strings.

In the initial learning stages, it is all right to imitate your favorite players for a few years, but ultimately you will have to set aside this behavior and strive to find the uniqueness in your own playing which you can expand upon and transmogrify as you explore and magnify every detail of your personality.

Pay attention to the choice of notes you are instantly drawn to when soloing, notice the different types of chord voicings you prefer, observe the way you perform bends and vibrato and how you strum funk rhythms and how you resolve tension in your licks.

Also, listening to as many different types and genres of music as possible will help you on your journey to developing your own style, since you will be more aware of the various 'sounds' available to you. Not to mention that it will help increase your appreciation for various kinds of music. Playing with other musicians as frequently as possible is also highly recommended. Jam with them in garages, bedrooms, and bars. Don't just sit in your room running scales and practicing extreme flashy techniques all day, go out into the real world and try to create phenomenal music with some actual musicians.

On Trios

I always liked bands that consisted of only three people. I preferred trios. Guitar, bass, drums. Simplicity. Occam's razor. Many musicians I ran into over the course of playing in bands and gigging did not like trios. They thought it produced a "thin" sound. They wanted two guitar players in the band. I did play in a couple of bands with two guitar players but it was not particularly fun for me. I would usually not be able to hear myself and the other guitarist and I would fight over volume levels. It was pretty frustrating.

I prefer the extra "space" that comes with trios because I feel it provides plenty of room for improvisation, which I have always loved. I also believe that the less musicians one has in a band, the "tighter" they will be as a group. By tight I mean that you will be able to communicate well through your instruments and be able to anticipate what the other players may do next and be able to follow them and stay together and make less mistakes overall as a cohesive unit. Being tight in a band is necessary and beneficial for producing good compelling music. In fact, if a trio plays together long enough, the group can almost develop a kind of mental telepathy. They can learn to read each other's minds in a way and anticipate what the other players will do with about a 70% success rate.

There were a few times when I didn't want to play in a trio. I wanted to add a brass instrument to the band. Mainly, I wanted to have a trumpet player. But I would have settled for other types of wind instruments such as a saxophone or a trombone. I thought adding only a single wind instrument would have greatly complimented our music. And the brass and the guitar could have done some exciting and zestful things together. We could have traded solos and played harmonized melodies together. Also I wanted to hear a wind instrument regularly since I knew it would affect my own phrasing during improvisations. Having a horn player would have changed how I played. I would have gotten out of the "guitar-thinking rut" and played more phrases similar to a horn. That would have been a great addition to the band, any band, but it never happened for me.

Back to trios. With them it is also easier to get everyone to come to rehearsals since there are less people. Getting band members to show up for rehearsals or engage in activities for which they receive little or no money is often exceedingly difficult, which you will soon find out when you join or form a band.

Ear Training

How can we improve our ears. How can we increase the accuracy of our sense of pitch. Good questions. Even if they don't have question marks. (I break a lot of rules in this book, I like breaking rules, you can break them too with your guitar, but learn a few first.) I do not believe there are any definitive answers for how to improve your ear for music, although I must admit I have never tried the perfect pitch courses advertised in many guitar magazines. Maybe they actually work, but I doubt it. (If any readers have ever tried them with success I would be interested in reading your accounts, my contact information is at the end of this book.)

Frankly, I was not born with the best set of ears in the world. I do not have perfect pitch, which is the ability to name correctly any note you hear. I can tune a guitar very quickly and I can recognize many types of chords by their sounds, e.g. I can easily tell the difference between a major chord and a major seventh chord, but during the beginning stages of learning how to play the guitar, I had trouble discerning guitar pitches enough that it affected my ability to tune the instrument (probably due to the cheap guitars I was learning to play on, which my father would give me after pulling them out of a dumpster in a back alley), keep in mind though that this was during my first couple of months of learning to play the guitar.

There are a few exercises you can try for improving your ear. Simple exercises that may or may not help you. I can't guarantee they will work, maybe a scientist would have to perform some case studies to be able to determine their level of efficacy, but anyway you can still try the exercises below. They surely won't hurt you.

1. Get a tape recorder and record some minor, major, minor 7th and major 7th chords with short pauses in between. Play them back and concentrate intensely on how they sound. Try to memorize the differences in overall tonality for each chord.

2. Now change keys and record different types of chords in this new key. Listen to them and again try to memorize each "character" and "flavor" of the chord. Listen as hard as you can, as closely as you can, try to absorb the identity of the chords.

3. Next, have a friend who can play guitar sit in a chair with her back to you. Ask her to play various chords that you tried to memorize earlier, but in a different key and completely random order without you being able to see your friend's hands. Once she plays a certain chord, try to name it. Ask her if you are correct. Keep going. Continue testing yourself, attempting to improve your ear. It doesn't matter if you get a lot of them wrong the first few times. Just don't get discouraged.

How to Become a Guitar Player from Hell

Once you have learned to recognize most of the more common chord types, try out a few atypical or unusual chords, such as suspended seconds, suspended fourths, augmented chords, ones with sharped sevenths and ninths, then after you think you have the flavors and overall tonalities of those chords memorized, have a friend test you by playing them with you trying to name the chords correctly.

You can move on to memorizing various scales and even individual notes afterward, trying to name them as well, although this type of ear training may be much more difficult. It is probably easier to name an entire tapestry of notes strummed together rather than identify a single note. But with practice I am sure you will be able to improve your ear for music in many areas, at least a small amount.

Original Riffs

Writing music, composing chord progressions and riffs, can be very rewarding (sometimes almost as stimulating as playing a great solo). After practicing for a couple of years you will probably find yourself making up little things on the guitar spontaneously. These may be riffs, chords, melodies, or short phrases, but what you are doing is composing your own music. Being creative is a good thing. You should always try to express yourself as much as possible, especially with the guitar.

Often people sit down to write music and succeed in inventing a couple of new things, but upon returning to them a few days later discover they no longer like what they originally wrote. This is common. Knowing what to throw away and what to keep is extremely important in the compositional process.

Below I have provided a very simple melody or riff of my own that I made up many years ago. Feel free to use it in any way you see fit. It is not especially great, but you can adapt it or modify it in any way you see fit.

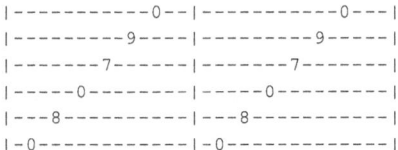

I would play the melody above by holding the chord (a simple E 7th Flat 9th chord) and simply strumming through it with a clean tone. It is not played in strict 8th notes, I normally strum some of the notes quicker than others, changing the rhythmic patterns and holding out the high E longer than the rest.

After a few repetitions of this I increase the speed of the strumming and add some distortion. Gradually I play it with a fully distorted tone and not allow the notes to ring out, as in an arpeggio. I like the riff because it sounds ominous. I would also play little fills such as sliding around on the high E string from the 7th to 12th to the 11th frets, and after another repetition of the riff I would insert this speedy large-interval tapping phrase:

```
      T              T
|-17-12-7-0-7-12-17-12-7-0---|
|----------------------------|
|----------------------------|
|----------------------------|
|----------------------------|
|----------------------------|
```

All notes above are either tapped, hammered or pulled. I would perform these fills between letting the high E ring out and then going back to the low E to start the arpeggio again.

I also have another simple blues groove I wish I could have included in this chapter, but the rhythms it contains make it especially hard to convey with tablature. Suffice it to say it's a simple groove played with E and A power chords and G and C notes on the third frets being bent up between transitions. The groove has a lot of "space" or rhythmic holes and is simple enough that most audiences really enjoy it. The riff is also perfect for adding in many fills and for playing solos over. I won't include it in this book but maybe that basic description will give you an idea for writing a similar groove of your own.

So there you have a couple of ideas for getting started composing your own original riffs for whenever the mood strikes you.

Out of the Box Exercise

The following is a philosophical or psychological guitar playing exercise that many might consider "off-the-wall" or highly unusual in nature. The more conservative readers should probably skip over this chapter as it is aimed at the more adventurous or frisky type of guitarists whoare willing to experiment and take chances or think differently, also the results of the exercise may not be entirely measureable.

Thinking out of the box. Playing out of the box. An out-of-the-box exercise that may make you feel like crawling inside a box or a refrigerator as soon as you are finished with it to escape any visionary or transcendental or outrageously zealous feelings you experience. Witness the sad blandishment. Thinking not playing, no, thinking and playing together, they go hand in hand out of a box or inside a despondent circle of freedom and you should

How to Become a Guitar Player from Hell

experiment with different methods you definitely need to try this one just feel it I said just feel those emotions washing over you as you attempt it and be assured this exercise will give you ultimate enlightenment and a shield against frivolity so lay back and open up your wise mind. A different type of exercise now, a different way to practice the guitar. Many of you will find it strange but it may help your playing and you may create something better than you ever expected something tremendous that you never thought possible. It is a philosophical or psychological exercise and it could be somewhat risky. Here it is.

1. Set up your guitar and amplifier in front of your favorite painting or a nice photograph that you like, or if you live in a scenic area you could simply look out your window, the main thing to do is choose a picture, sculpture or scene, some type of visually stimulating work that inspires you. It could be an avant-garde painting or a picture of a pirate or photo of your grandparents, anything so long as it produces some kind of feeling inside you whenever you observe its details and qualities.

2. Start playing whatever comes into your mind, but try to play what you see in front of you. Attempt to recreate audibly the images you are observing, try to create sounds you think represent the picture you're looking at.

3. Observe well and take in all subtleties and vicissitudes and stylistic embellishments of the painting or scene and let them come out of your hands by playing your guitar. Take in the visual information, whatever it may be, and let it reintegrate and flow into the core of your being and filter it through your mind and personality and spirit and release it to describe what your eyes take in and make your fingers manipulate the auditory expression of the scene through music by playing a solo or riff or set of chord changes with your guitar. Anything that represents and describes the image with sound.

That is the exercise. An out of the box exercise. Nothing to it. No right or wrong. Try it and see if you can represent a picture that inspires you with music. Make melodies that describe the entire image, even if they are merely abstractions of an avant-garde painting. It will be interesting. If you attempt this exercise you will be breaking out of the normal confines of guitar practice and it is always profitable to try different ways of practicing to penetrate other planes of existence. Attempt to rise above the mundane. A guitar player in our modern world must do everything she can, she must try every technique in the book and some that haven't even been invented yet to arrive at her own style of playing and stand above the millions of other guitarists in the world. Will you stand out I hope you can I think you can do it I hope you at least try.

Remember that the goal of the instructional material and each of the exercises in this book is to help you achieve your own individuality, to learn how to express the music naturally occuring within you. It will be propitious to try different exercises and believe in them enough and in what they can do for you and also to believe in yourself enough to make a difference, if you can do that it will help your proficiency on the instrument substantially yes it will definitely. Try it give it a chance just one chance, please do not be put off by this out-of-the-box psychological or philosophical exercise because it is interesting and you may create some very good music by attempting it.

Finding the Right Key to Solo In

Occasionally you may find yourself in a situation where someone in your band has written a song and they expect you to solo over a set of chord changes but they are not familiar enough with music theory to let you know what key the song is in. I will tell you how to find the main key or mode to any song based on any set of chord changes so that when someone presents you with a strange tune you can solo your ass off with no worries.

1) Write down all the chords you are expected to solo over. For illustration purposes, let's say your set of chords is something simple such as, G, Bmin7, Emin.

2) Since you know the names of the notes on all parts of the fretboard, and the songwriter in your band has shown you the exact voicings of the chords you will be using, it will be easy for you to write down the notes that make up the chords as they are to be played in the song. In our example above, the notes in our chord progression when written out become:

G chord: G, B, D, G, D, G
Bmin7: B, F#, A, D, F#
Emin: E, B, E, G, B, E

3) Next, write down the notes that occur in the chords in order from A to G, eliminating any repeats, like this: A, B, D, E, F#, G.

4) Now it will take a little bit of trial and error, but begin by playing through the notes above and looking for any patterns that resemble scales you already know. Even if you are only fluent in a few of the most common scales you should recognize at least one pattern before long. Concerning our example, after some experimentation you will probably notice that the B, D, E, and F# notes are the beginning of the B minor pentatonic scale. Let's look at that more closely. Since the G is added afterward, notice that it resembles a standard B minor scale. And if you add in the C note, you will quickly realize the correct key to use over the chords is B minor. Notice that C did not appear among the notes listed for our chord progression above. But by playing it you

can hear that it fits well. Hence, our example chord changes are in the key of B minor, or D major, which is equivalent.

Once you have the key established you can use the rest of the modes you know from memorizing C major over the entire fretboard and simply move them up a whole step. Doing this reveals that you can play D major or D Ionian over our {G, Bmin7, Emin} progression, and also E Dorian, or F# Phrygian, or C# Lydian, etcetera. You can also add in as many outside notes as possible so that the main scale or overall tonality doesn't even matter anymore and you can simply flail your fingers around atonally using the strangest patterns you can think of and then claim you are the greatest avant-garde musician since Ornette Coleman. (Just kidding about that last sentence.)

So that's all there is to discovering the correct key to solo over when all you have is a set of chord changes to go by. Just write down the notes directly from the chord progression and see which scales they naturally match up with. It's kids' stuff.

On Performing Live

The title of this chapter could also be 'What Not to Do When Performing Live.' You see, there are many poseurs in the rock world. These are people who pretend they are "feeling" the music and then perform contrived gestures and pose a lot when in fact they are not really feeling anything at all and it is easily apparent that their ridiculous movements and emotions are fake. They may fool a few people, but they don't fool many.

Please don't pose. Please do not pretend that you are feeling things on stage when you're really not. Don't fake anything. When you get up there, just act as naturally as possible. If your band is playing a song that you don't particularly enjoy or you do not feel anything special when creating the music, the best thing to do is simply stand there and not move a muscle except in your hands, forearms and fingers and just concentrate on playing your guitar the best you can. Some people may call you boring but believe me it is much better to stay still than dance or flop around and headbang, pretending you are feeling incredibly overwhelming emotion from the music when you're really not feeling a damn thing and you just took some crappy drama classes a few years earlier and posing is how the goofy acting teacher expected you to act when pretending to be in a rock band. Everyone watching you is going to know you're faking it. Believe me, people aren't stupid. They'll know. So don't fake it. Feel it. And if you don't, refrain from posing or acting at all. Contrived moves such as exaggerated lip puckering or excessive hip shaking and dancing or running around smiling and blowing kisses to the gorgeous women in the audience are activities to be avoided if you worked them out beforehand.

I have been in a lot of bands with many poseurs. It is for the most part excruciating. I also see a lot of fakers on reality television shows in which famous bands are looking for rock singers. Some of these so-called musicians are obviously actors with many years of drama classes behind them and one day they awoke and heard about an audition to be a rock singer and decided to try out and then proceeded to pose their butts off like morons in front of millions of people. It is quite disgusting and nauseating but also a wonderful thing that none of these actors ever win the competition in the end. People know when you are posing and when you are genuinely feeling the music. Come on. Don't kid yourself.

Of course you can respond to music in any manner you choose but I feel it is best to let things come from your heart and soul and respond honestly to any music around you.

Some Necessary Tools for Working on Your Guitar

You may need to make a few slight repairs on your guitar during a live situation, or need to make a few adjustments at rehearsal or at home. Below are a few essential tools you should keep in your guitar case, or even in a small tool box in the trunk of your car, at all times. Many common repairs for the guitar are simple ones, but you will definitely need the proper tool for the job. If you are playing a paying gig it is absolutely imperative you bring with you most of the tools in the following list since you are now a serious professional guitarist who needs to show proper responsibility. You don't want to be caught in a desperate situation in front of hundreds of people without the necessary tools to fix a problem with your equipment.

1) Picks – keep many extras handy, put them in your guitar case or your shoes or under your hat; picks are quite disposable and you should purchase them by the pound.

2) Strings – at least two extra sets of strings will be necessary; breaking strings is quite common, especially live.

3) Extra cords – a noisy cord with a short in it is no good when you're playing mega-decibels through a Marshall stack.

4) Tuner – although not absolutely necessary, they are nice to have for tuning quietly.

5) Batteries – for your effects pedals, if you use them; two 9-volt batteries and several AAs should do the trick.

6) Pliers – standard and needle nose; for general repairs, things like digging out broken string remnants from tuning posts, etc.

How to Become a Guitar Player from Hell

7) Screwdrivers – for adjusting the bridge of your guitar or strap, and maybe for working on your amp.

8) Pen & paper – for jotting down licks that come into your head at weird moments; writing down a hilarious joke someone told you in an alley on a break that you want to tell your uncle; a nice chord voicing you didn't realize was possible; writing down directions to a strip club after the gig, etc.

9) Flashlight – for when you have to conduct surgery on your instrument in a dark club; or to find your contact lense that flew out while you were head banging with the bass player.

10) Duct tape – always useful for anything and everything.

So there you have a few essential and not so essential tools that can help you repair a lot of problems that may arise during your professional guitar playing career. They may even become genuine life savers at some point. If you are getting paid to play for people, you need to put on your best performance, as free from down time and glitches and equipment failures as possible, so be sure to have the right tools at your disposal.

Imitation & Call and Response

I am writing this short chapter while sitting at a picnic table in front of a vacant concession stand that is surrounded by four empty baseball fields. A large blackbird is perched on a telephone wire above me and we are engaged in a sort of "call and response." First, the blackbird makes a noise: "Squawk-eech-eech-eech." Then I try to echo the same sounds back to him. I can see the bird listening to my response, then he pauses for a moment and changes his call to a different one, "Thwack-tee-too, tee-too, thwack- tee-too." The blackbirds in this area of Texas can make a wide range of bizarre sound effects, some of them quite surprising and even a little scary.

(Call and response is usually a type of interaction between a person and a group in which a statement is made and any type of response, verbal or nonverbal, can be sounded back as a kind of "answer" to the initial call. It doesn't have to be an exact echoing of the caller's original words.)

This encounter with the musical blackbird reminds me of an unusual yet effective practice method whereby one tries to imitate noises or sounds with their guitar, sounds one would normally not even attempt to play. Bird calls, elephant blasts, loud sirens, robotic or computer sounds from old sci-fi movies, death rattles, powerful engines, chainsaws, women or old men screaming, any kind of sound at all can be fruitful for you to imitate on your guitar. Not only will this improve your technique considerably, it may also prod you to begin thinking outside the limited guitar-based mindset. Many guitarists get wrapped up and pigeonholed into playing only what they have heard other guitar players perform. You should avoid that.

One sound effect I enjoyed trying to replicate on guitar in my early days was the sound of a bumblebee stinging a person. I would use a lot of exaggerated tremolo bar vibrato on lower notes on the G string to imitate the bumblebee buzzing around, then hit a high harmonic and yank it upward with my tremolo bar to represent the sting, then I'd hit a low note and depress the bar to represent the pain the person felt. Try it out if you like.

You should also listen to many different types of music and try to play things that seem very difficult or even impossible and allow the process to change the way you think about your instrument.

To slightly return to the topic of this chapter, when playing blues, you can perform "question-and-answer" phrasing, where you initiate a phrase and end it first in a high pitched manner (question), then play the same beginning again but give it a lower pitched ending (the answer), which may be considered another form of call and response.

Improving Your Sense of Rhythm

Having good timing and a strong sense of rhythm is invaluable if you want to become a true guitar player from hell. Some people are born with excellent innate senses of rhythm while others are not. Here is an experiment you can perform if you like: find a person with good rhythm and play them a bluesy groove and see if they immediately start moving their hips and swaying to the rhythm of the music; then play the song for a person with no innate sense of rhythm and see if they just stand there, totally lifeless, with a perplexed look on their face. If you ask the person with no rhythm to start dancing to the song, they might sling their arms and legs around in a herky-jerky fashion, which could remind you of a person falling down a well or having a seizure. I am not making fun of these people. It is just the difference between having a natural sense of rhythm and not having one.

Personally, I was born with a fairly decent sense of rhythm, while my father was not. He simply cannot feel where the beat should be in songs. I don't know the reason beind it, but it isn't his fault. He has learned to play the guitar moderately well but quite robotically over the years even though he has no natural sense of rhythm, so there is a little hope for others. At first my father would play riffs and songs totally out of time, but now he has improved his rhythm considerably, although you can still tell he does not have a natural feel for where the beat should be. Again, this means there is hope for other players born without a natural sense of timing.

How to Become a Guitar Player from Hell

Don't get discouraged if your body wasn't blessed with a natural feel for rhythm, don't smash your guitar against your refrigerator if someone says you are playing out of time, because I have a few ideas that may be able to help you. I am not sure how many of them will actually work because they have never been tested. But I feel the suggestions below must have some value since they each involve working with rhythm in some way and involve large amounts of common sense. I have never read about any tried-and-true methods that definitely enhance one's sense of time. If I would have, I would've listed them here. Nevertheless, here are a few suggestions:

1. Buy a metronome.

2. When practicing a song or various riffs, always use your metronome and make a conscious effort to play in time with the beat while asking yourself if you're playing with the proper rhythm.

3. Jam along to as many CDs as you can, always trying to feel the beat of the drummer and staying in exact synchronization with the guitars.

4. Learn how to play the drums. If you can't afford to purchase an entire set, you could buy some of those small electronic practice pads, or make your own crude drum set from cardboard boxes or other items around your house.

5. Take dance lessons from a top-level instructor. (I am not joking here. Although I have never tried it, it doesn't seem like a bad idea.) Ask the instructor to explain the concept of rhythm to you, ask them how you can improve your own natural sense of timing. They may have the perfect answer.

To reiterate, a couple of the methods above are untested, but even if you try them and they are not supremely effective I am sure none of them would make your sense of rhythm any worse. I hope at least a few of the ideas help.

How to Get Gigs

Once your band has been practicing for a few months (and hopefully your other members had a certain level of playing experience before you got together) and you have worked up at least 40 songs – both original and covers – you will probably want to get a gig somewhere. I mean, what good is being in a band if you don't get to play live and go berserk rolling around on stage flailing on your guitar while spewing whiskey out of your mouth to impress members of the opposite sex (J. K.). Of course you can play at parties for your friends and that is probably the best way to begin, but say you are past that stage and ready to get some professional experience and you would also like to get paid for your efforts (even though a hundred bucks split four ways won't even come close to covering the cost of your guitar strings for the last few months) and you would like to have people other than your personal friends hear your band.

How to Become a Guitar Player from Hell

For a few of the bands I was in, we would drive around looking for bars, go in and ask the owner if they wanted to hire a band. Most would give us a gig automatically if we told them we had already performed a few times at other bars in the general area, while others would ask for a "promo-pack," which is usually a press kit containing a photo of the band, a one-page biography, a demo tape, a list of songs, press clippings, etc. (No band I was ever in had a promo pack.) On other occasions I would simply look up bars in the phone book, call them up and ask if they featured live music, then tell them I was in a band and name some other bars we had played, then ask if we could set a date for a gig. Simple as that. It worked many times. I got plenty of gigs this way, although we never got paid much.

I should mention that these methods probably only work for bars that want you to play other artist's material – I was mainly in cover bands, although we would always work in a few of our original songs. In bigger cities I realize there are clubs where they want bands to play only their original music, but I was never fortunate enough to play in a club of this type. We always played four, 45-minute sets, usually from around nine PM to one PM, but occasionally until two. The most money any band I was in ever received was $365, but usually our pay would only be around $100 to $200. So don't do it for the money at the beginning. Of course if you get lucky and establish yourself later on as an excellent band and get a fan following, no matter how small, you may work up to getting paid a fairly decent amount for a gig compared to the time you put in: a few thousand dollars.

If you are planning on being a cover band (which you should do for at least a while in the beginning), you will need a good mixture of songs. Blues, pop, rock, metal, and also try to get a couple of current songs off the radio, the most popular material possible, whether it be rock, metal or whatever your taste, you should learn the songs people are currently listening to and singing in their cars. Usually these tunes will not be too difficult to learn by ear, or the tablature for some may appear in the current guitar magazines.

Guitar Related Quotes

Quotes by famous guitar players, or quotes about playing the guitar itself, can occasionally be inspiring and fun to recite. During my early years of playing guitar, when that was the only thing in the world I lived for, sometimes I would lie in bed at night and ponder a particular phrase spoken by one of my favorite guitar heroes as I tried to fall asleep.

Here are some of my favorite quotes by well-known guitarists or quotes concerning playing the guitar itself. Maybe a couple of them will inspire you in some way.

How to Become a Guitar Player from Hell

"The guitar is a small orchestra. It is polyphonic. Every string is a different color, a different voice."
– Andre Segovia

"You have to know a song so well, that while you are playing it, if someone were to blow your head off with a double-barrelled shotgun, your body would still finish the song."
– Stefan Grossman (paraphrased)

"We didn't have any instruments, so I had to use my guitar."
– Mother Maybelle Carter

"My guitar is not a thing. It is an extension of myself. It is who I am."
– Joan Jett

"Puberty was very vague. I literally locked myself in a room and played guitar."
– Johnny Depp (Depp was a guitarist in a moderately successful band before becoming an uber-successful movie star and sex symbol.)

"I was left with an urge to make the guitar sound like things it shouldn't be able to sound like."
– Adrian Belew

"I can't do anything but play guitar."
– Tommy Bolin

"Lean your body forward slightly to support the guitar against your chest, for the poetry of the music should resound in your heart."
– Andre Segovia

"My vocation is more in composition really than anything else – building up harmonies using the guitar, orchestrating the guitar like an army, a guitar army."
– Jimmy Page

"Enthusiasm is everything. It must be taut and vibrating like a guitar string."
– Pele (The Brazilian soccer player.)

How to Become a Guitar Player from Hell

"Passing the vodka bottle. And playing the guitar."
— Keith Richards (His answer to how he stays in good physical shape.)

"Shut Up 'n' Play Yer Guitar"
— Frank Zappa (Title of one of his albums.)

Start A Revolution With Your Guitar

(Warning: The following is another unusual "thinking" or "philosophical" or "outside-the-box" lesson).

You may want to start a revolutionary movement with your guitar. The methods and techniques you have learned in this book could help you demolish the normal standards of guitar playing once you have worked through them, mastered them, and then taken them to another level. One of the things you will have to do to start a revolution is learn to play with absolute conviction and confidence and be exceptionally aggressive – never be docile in your playing (unless the music truly calls for it). Attempt to take your music into the metaphysical realm and change the world with your solos and chord progressions. You will need genuine pugnacity and ferocity, arrogance and even a little belligerence to accomplish this, to burst into the supernatural plane with your music.

Developing a strong urge to destroy the traditional boundaries of harmony with the sounds coming from your guitar will be propitious to your revolutionary movement. You could try to find the 5th and 11th dimensions with your lyrical and pointillistic improvisations and bring the dimensions back to us and reveal their esoteric qualities to your audience. You could be the first guitar player on the planet to capture an extra dimension and present it to the common people, which would definitely cause a revolution in music and you would go down in history for it. We need more revolutions.

Every musician and guitarist should attempt to make radical changes in music with their playing. They should create new music that drives people into deep religious ecstasy, causes people to riot in the streets and the cities to crumble and planets to spin backwards on their axes. Your new music should be able to heal the sick and the elderly and the mentally ill, and make other individuals turn into mystics who strive for the forbidden, and cause other people to have terrifying existential meltdowns. It wouldn't hurt too much and you would change the world. Wouldn't you like to create anarchy in the streets with your riffs and feedback and other sounds coming from your guitar. Wouldn't you like to make the universe burn from within and bring about the apocalypse. Try it. Nobody will get hurt too bad.

How to Become a Guitar Player from Hell

Attempt to arrive at a level of reality that human beings rarely if ever witness, try to reach the mystical realm lying beyond the common veil of the universe, do it with your guitar and bring the ultimate level of reality back to us, show it to us, the incomprehensible level of existence and the blistering essence we all know is there but rarely get to experience. There is a curtain over it a barrier maybe even a brick wall. You must break it down bust through it get to that other realm with your performances. It is possible. There is music there. Hiding and slinking. It might be impossible for some players to find it but I believe you can do it so you should attempt to do so. The greatest music in the world lies in that metaphysical region. You simply have to capture it with your guitar and improvisations and bring it out. I am talking about the almost incomprehensible level of reality residing just outside the barriers of our visual perception, you can feel it sometimes, a few people can, you should try to reach it, bring it out of its hiding place.

Just as superstring physicists believe we live in eleven dimensions or more, just as they believe tiny strings are vibrating to make up everything we know in the universe and all matter as we experience it, I would like for you to get the strings of your guitar vibrating in perfect synchronicity with the superstrings of the universe and bring out the music it contains, the true music, the genuine music, so you will be at one with the superstrings of the universe. It is attainable. Bring out the clandestine music in the realms beyond our senses. Go into the pleroma, bring back the melodies residing there. Make us believe in the mystical transport possible through music. The truly real, supernatural transport, bring it back to us. Use your guitar. Take us to another realm with your playing and cause people to create religious cults devoted to your music. One way to do that is to become provocative. Let your guitar become provocative. Your fingers hands and mind all provocative. Your soul ears limbs facial features eyes everything provocative. Try to express the ineffable with your improvisations and arrive at the sublime truth. Take us deep into the pleroma. Make us fly. Keep your strings in motion with the superstrings of the universe. How many superstrings does it take to make up the vibrating note of an F# played on your high E string? You tell me, discover the answer.

Now, do the suggestions I wrote above seem supremely strange or totally out-there? Does it seem like I am only joking or off my rocker or have my tongue firmly planted in my cheek? Some of the things I listed may sound crazy or bizarre but there is a reason and method behind the madness. (You might think this lesson is entirely too strange or even ridiculous and that is why I put it near the end of this book, in case it was too wild you wouldn't quit reading in the middle.) But the important thing here is, most of your guitar playing and improvisations come from your mind. So if you change the way you think about your instrument and how you approach the performance of a piece of music, it will alter the way you play. Having certain thoughts or feelings in mind before you make music, having certain philosophical goals or psychological theories in your head beforehand will affect your playing tremendously and may even take it to a level you never thought possible. That is what you want. Strive for the impossible. Aim beyond yourself. Go into the beyond. Try to take your playing to places no one has ever dreamed of. Good luck with your attempts.

Two Useful Software Tools

Below are two wonderful tools that helped me immensely in the writing of this book.

1. *Chord Search Engine* at http://jguitar.com/

This wonderful web site allows you to find and name any type of chord or scale. Some of the incredibly useful programs freely available are Chord Namer, Scale Calculator, and Tab Mapper, among others.

2. *Power Tab Editor* at http://www.power-tab.net/

This is a free program that allows you to write music by entering tablature into an editor, which you can then listen to via MIDI technology. The *Power Tab Editor* is a powerful compositional tool capable of producing sophisticated music or just simple guitar licks. The interface is intuitive and the program easy to learn, while also being very educational.

If you would like to hear any of the tablature featured in this book, or see what the standard musical notation for it looks like, simply download the *Power Tab Editor* and type in the numbers in the tab I've provided for the various lessons. The traditional musical notation will appear as you are typing and to hear it simply press the play button.

In Summary

So there you have it. That is almost everything I know about playing the guitar, or at least most of what I can remember at this point in my life. I tried to get the gist of every major topic down for your individual use. I tried to discuss everything that constituted my being considered a guitar player from hell by one individual a few years ago.

If you have read this book from the first page to the last then you could say you know every one of my "secret" techniques that set me apart as a guitar player, and if you played through each method and concept I discussed then you also heard them as well. I hope you thought they were helpful and you learned something and that the musical examples sounded decent and interesting.

I attempted to give you knowledge that was useful and I tried to give you plenty of unusual tips and information to take your guitar playing to another level, I tried to give you most of the techniques that make up the extent of my rock, metal, and blues guitar style. Perhaps you learned quite a few things you were not familiar with before, I hope you did and that the methods allowed you to become more proficient on the guitar.

As I stated in the preface, my main goal in each chapter was to present you with the basics and then add extra bits of knowledge that I had never seen discussed anywhere else so you could save a lot of time by not having to discover them yourself. Almost every guitarist who has been playing for years could give you plenty of tips and information concerning "secret" techniques or methods they have discovered through experimentation and rehearsals and live gig experience, I wanted to share mine by writing this book.

Perhaps someday you too will be playing a gig somewhere and an anonymous person will walk up and say that you sound like a guitar player from hell. If that happens then this book will have served its purpose.

But the techniques and advice listed in this book are not the end. In fact, they are only the beginning. An infinite amount of discovery is still ahead of you. The most important thing any guitar player can do is continue striving for sounds they hear in their head and develop their technique enough to realize them so they can develop their own style of playing and create their own voice instantly recognizeable to others and one that will be a genuine vehicle for self-expression. Strive to develop your technique to its utmost extent and explore your personality and individuality so you will be able to play anything and everything you feel. That is really all a guitar player can ever hope to achieve.

Thank you for reading this book.

Goodbye and good luck with your guitar playing.

THE END

About the Author

Jason Earls has over twenty years experience playing electric and acoustic guitar. He started at the age of 14 and began playing in bands from the time he knew three chords and the minor pentatonic scale. The names of some of his bands were *Anathema, Tainted Angel, Jack Nasty, The Grinning Cynics, Underfire, The Blue Druds, Sergio and the Comancheros, Vestigial Speculation, Dunor's Stupid Band, Mama Cheetah, The Kitchen Gods*, and others.

In addition to being an avid guitar player, Jason Earls is a writer and computational number theorist whose fiction and nonfiction has been published in *Thirteen, Red Scream, MathWorld.com, Neometropolis, Bust Down the Door and Eat All the Chickens, Scientia Magna, Escaping Elsewhere, Theatre of Decay, The Online Encyclopedia of Integer Sequences*, and other publications. He is also the author of the novels, *Red Zen, 0.13610152128364555667891l...* and *If(Sid_Vicious == TRUE && Alan_Turing == TRUE) {ERROR_Cyberpunk();}* as well as *Cocoon of Terror*, which will be published by Afterbirth Books in 2007.

Contact: jcearls@cableone.net

Special thanks to Christine Earls, Scene Williams, Dorlynn Earls, and Chad Ian Earls.

About the Artist

Cover art by Jason Daniels.
Award winning Animator and Artist,
Graduated with a Degree in animation 2006.
Jase likes filth and weirdos.
He lives off a diet of nicotine, peanut butter
and anxiety.
To see more of his work visit:
www.jasedaniels.com
Contact:
mail@jasedaniels.com
jason2019@hotmail.com
http://www.myspace.com/jasedaniels

www.ingramcontent.com/pod-product-compliance
Lightning Source LLC
Chambersburg PA
CBHW032048090426
42744CB00004B/127